Angels
Address Book

TELEGRAPH ROAD

TELEGRAPH ROAD

Address Book

First published in 2003 by Telegraph Road
©Telegraph Road

It was the intention of Telegraph Road to capture the essence and spirit of what has been said about Angels. While every effort has been made to determine the original source of the quotes used in this book and attribute them accordingly, the internet is a flawed document and may have taken liberties and paraphrased for its own purposes

This edition was published by Telegraph Road
ISBN: 0-9733107-7-4

Cover, interior design & layout: Lawrie Korec

Concept: Ronald Goelman

For bulk purchases please contact:
sales@telegraph-rd.com

For other inquiries please contact:
inquiries@telegraph-rd.com

Telegraph Road
36 Northline Road
Toronto, Ontario, Canada   M4B 3E2

PRINTED IN CHINA

Cover image: Angel Musician (fresco) by Melozzo da Forli (1438-94)
©Vatican Museums and Galleries, Vatican City, Italy/Bridgeman Art Library
An Angel Playing a Flageolet (w/c) by Sir Edward Burne-Jones (1833-98)
©Private Collection/Bridgeman Art Library

*Sometimes our reason for hope
rests on the wings of angels.*

They hear our pleas, musings and prayers and become our messengers. Angels are the vehicle that can allow our dreams to take flight and break free. Without angels our lives are but brief, fleeting moments of time caught in the maelstrom of chaos. We feel their motion in the darkness and hear the faint flutter of their wings in our deepest times of doubt. And while we occupy with them that landscape that falls between temptation and redemption, they do not lead us nor do they follow us, but together with us, strive to approach the Divine.

– Georges Luis Guevara

Emergency Numbers and Personal Information

DRIVING INFORMATION

Car Make and Model _____

License Plate _____

Registration _____

Driver's License # _____

Insurance Policy # _____

Insurance Company Phone _____

Insurance Agent _____

HEALTH INSURANCE

Insurance Company Phone _____

Insurance Policy # _____

Insurance Agent _____

Phone _____

FREQUENTLY DIALED NUMBERS

Babysitter _____

Pharmacy _____

Electrician _____

Computer Technician _____

Plumber _____

_____

_____

_____

_____

Personal Contact Numbers

PERSONAL INFORMATION

Name _____

Address _____

_____

_____

Home Phone _____

Cell _____

Vacation Home Phone _____

Email _____

BUSINESS INFORMATION

Business Address _____

Phone _____

Fax _____

Email _____

NOTIFY IN CASE OF EMERGENCY

Name _____

Relationship _____

Address _____

_____

_____

Home Phone _____

Work Phone _____

Cell _____

Name _____

Address _____

_____

Home _____ Work _____

Cell _____ Email _____

Name _____

Address _____

_____

Home _____ Work _____

Cell _____ Email _____

Name _____

Address _____

_____

Home _____ Work _____

Cell _____ Email _____

Name _____

Address _____

_____

Home _____ Work _____

Cell _____ Email _____

Name _____

Address _____

_____

Home _____ Work _____

Cell _____ Email _____

Angels are intelligent reflections of light, that original light which has no beginning. They can illuminate. They do not need tongues or ears for they can communicate without speech in thought.

— St. John of Damascus

Name _____

Address _____

_____

Home _____ Work _____

Cell _____ Email _____

<hr />

Name _____

Address _____

_____

Home _____ Work _____

Cell _____ Email _____

<hr />

Name _____

Address _____

_____

Home _____ Work _____

Cell _____ Email _____

<hr />

Name _____

Address _____

_____

Home _____ Work _____

Cell _____ Email _____

Name _____

Address _____

_____

Home _____ Work _____

Cell _____ Email _____

Name _____

Address _____

_____

Home _____ Work _____

Cell _____ Email _____

Name _____

Address _____

_____

Home _____ Work _____

Cell _____ Email _____

Name _____

Address _____

_____

Home _____ Work _____

Cell _____ Email _____

Name _____

Address _____

_____

Home _____ Work _____

Cell _____ Email _____

Name _____

Address _____

_____

Home _____ Work _____

Cell _____ Email _____

Name _____

Address _____

_____

Home _____ Work _____

Cell _____ Email _____

Name _____

Address _____

_____

Home _____ Work _____

Cell _____ Email _____

Name _____

Address _____

_____

Home _____ Work _____

Cell _____ Email _____

Make yourself familiar with the angels, and behold them frequently in spirit;
for without being seen, they are present with you.

— Saint Francis de Sales

A

Name _____

Address _____

_____

Home _____ Work _____

Cell _____ Email _____

Name _____

Address _____

_____

Home _____ Work _____

Cell _____ Email _____

Name _____

Address _____

_____

Home _____ Work _____

Cell _____ Email _____

Name _____

Address _____

_____

Home _____ Work _____

Cell _____ Email _____

Name _____

Address _____

_____

Home _____ Work _____

Cell _____ Email _____

B

Name _____

Address _____

_____

Home _____ Work _____

Cell _____ Email _____

Name _____

Address _____

_____

Home _____ Work _____

Cell _____ Email _____

Name _____

Address _____

_____

Home _____ Work _____

Cell _____ Email _____

Name _____

Address _____

_____

Home _____ Work _____

Cell _____ Email _____

I went forth to find an angel
And found this effort brought
That life is full of so much good
The touch that angels wrought.

– James Joseph Huesgen

B

Name

Address

Home   Work

Cell   Email

Name

Address

Home   Work

Cell   Email

Name

Address

Home   Work

Cell   Email

Name

Address

Home   Work

Cell   Email

Name

Address

Home   Work

Cell   Email

Name _____

Address _____

_____

Home _____ Work _____

Cell _____ Email _____

Name _____

Address _____

_____

Home _____ Work _____

Cell _____ Email _____

Name _____

Address _____

_____

Home _____ Work _____

Cell _____ Email _____

Name _____

Address _____

_____

Home _____ Work _____

Cell _____ Email _____

Angels are spirits, but it is not because they are spirits that they are Angels. They become Angels when they are sent. For the name Angel refers to their office, not their nature. You ask the name of this nature, it is spirit; you ask its office, it is that of an Angel, which is a messenger.

— St. Augustine

C

Name _____

Address _____

_____

Home _____ Work _____

Cell _____ Email _____

Name _____

Address _____

_____

Home _____ Work _____

Cell _____ Email _____

Name _____

Address _____

_____

Home _____ Work _____

Cell _____ Email _____

Name _____

Address _____

_____

Home _____ Work _____

Cell _____ Email _____

Name _____

Address _____

_____

Home _____ Work _____

Cell _____ Email _____

Look homeward Angel now and melt with Ruth.

— John Milton

Name _____

Address _____

_____

Home _____ Work _____

Cell _____ Email _____

Name _____

Address _____

_____

Home _____ Work _____

Cell _____ Email _____

Name _____

Address _____

_____

Home _____ Work _____

Cell _____ Email _____

Name _____

Address _____

_____

Home _____ Work _____

Cell _____ Email _____

C

Name _____

Address _____

_____

Home _____ Work _____

Cell _____ Email _____

Name _____

Address _____

_____

Home _____ Work _____

Cell _____ Email _____

Name _____

Address _____

_____

Home _____ Work _____

Cell _____ Email _____

Name _____

Address _____

_____

Home _____ Work _____

Cell _____ Email _____

Name _____

Address _____

_____

Home _____ Work _____

Cell _____ Email _____

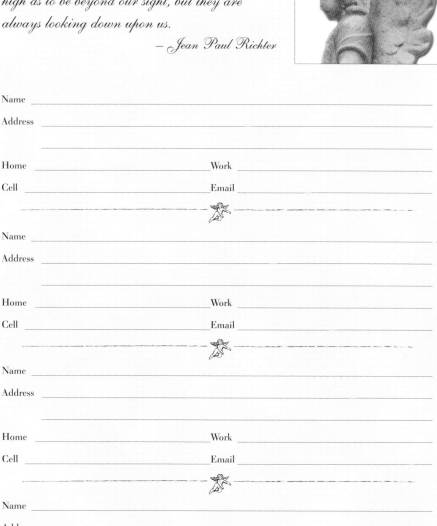

The guardian angels of life sometimes fly so high as to be beyond our sight, but they are always looking down upon us.

— Jean Paul Richter

D

Name _____

Address _____

_____

Home _____ Work _____

Cell _____ Email _____

Name _____

Address _____

_____

Home _____ Work _____

Cell _____ Email _____

Name _____

Address _____

_____

Home _____ Work _____

Cell _____ Email _____

Name _____

Address _____

_____

Home _____ Work _____

Cell _____ Email _____

D

Name

Address

Home   Work

Cell   Email

Name

Address

Home   Work

Cell   Email

Name

Address

Home   Work

Cell   Email

Name

Address

Home   Work

Cell   Email

Name

Address

Home   Work

Cell   Email

Name _____

Address _____

_____

Home _____ Work _____

Cell _____ Email _____

Name _____

Address _____

_____

Home _____ Work _____

Cell _____ Email _____

Name _____

Address _____

_____

Home _____ Work _____

Cell _____ Email _____

Name _____

Address _____

_____

Home _____ Work _____

Cell _____ Email _____

Thou fair-hair'd angel of the evening,
Now, whilst the sun rests on the mountains, light
Thy bright torch of love; thy radiant crown
Put on, and smile upon our evening bed!

— William Blake

Name _____

Address _____

_____

Home _____ Work _____

Cell _____ Email _____

Name _____

Address _____

_____

Home _____ Work _____

Cell _____ Email _____

Name _____

Address _____

_____

Home _____ Work _____

Cell _____ Email _____

Name _____

Address _____

_____

Home _____ Work _____

Cell _____ Email _____

Name _____

Address _____

_____

Home _____ Work _____

Cell _____ Email _____

For fools rush in where angels fear to tread.
— *Alexander Pope*

Name _____

Address _____

_____

Home _____ Work _____

Cell _____ Email _____

Name _____

Address _____

_____

Home _____ Work _____

Cell _____ Email _____

Name _____

Address _____

_____

Home _____ Work _____

Cell _____ Email _____

Name _____

Address _____

_____

Home _____ Work _____

Cell _____ Email _____

Name _____

Address _____

_____

Home _____ Work _____

Cell _____ Email _____

Name _____

Address _____

_____

Home _____ Work _____

Cell _____ Email _____

Name _____

Address _____

_____

Home _____ Work _____

Cell _____ Email _____

Name _____

Address _____

_____

Home _____ Work _____

Cell _____ Email _____

Name _____

Address _____

_____

Home _____ Work _____

Cell _____ Email _____

Name _____

Address _____

_____

Home _____ Work _____

Cell _____ Email _____

Name _____

Address _____

_____

Home _____ Work _____

Cell _____ Email _____

Name _____

Address _____

_____

Home _____ Work _____

Cell _____ Email _____

Name _____

Address _____

_____

Home _____ Work _____

Cell _____ Email _____

The golden moments in the stream of life rush past us and we see nothing but sand; the angels come to visit us, and we only know them when they are gone.

— George Eliot

Name _____

Address _____

_____

Home _____ Work _____

Cell _____ Email _____

Name _____

Address _____

_____

Home _____ Work _____

Cell _____ Email _____

Name _____

Address _____

_____

Home _____ Work _____

Cell _____ Email _____

Name _____

Address _____

_____

Home _____ Work _____

Cell _____ Email _____

Name _____

Address _____

_____

Home _____ Work _____

Cell _____ Email _____

Name _____

Address _____

_____

Home _____ Work _____

Cell _____ Email _____

Name _____

Address _____

_____

Home _____ Work _____

Cell _____ Email _____

Name _____

Address _____

_____

Home _____ Work _____

Cell _____ Email _____

Name _____

Address _____

_____

Home _____ Work _____

Cell _____ Email _____

The virtue of angels is that they cannot deteriorate; their flaw is that they cannot improve.
Man's flaw is that he can deteriorate; and his virtue is that he can improve.

— The Talmud

Name

Address

Home   Work

Cell   Email

Name

Address

Home   Work

Cell   Email

Name

Address

Home   Work

Cell   Email

Name

Address

Home   Work

Cell   Email

Name

Address

Home   Work

Cell   Email

Name _____

Address _____

_____

Home _____ Work _____

Cell _____ Email _____

Name _____

Address _____

_____

Home _____ Work _____

Cell _____ Email _____

Name _____

Address _____

_____

Home _____ Work _____

Cell _____ Email _____

Name _____

Address _____

_____

Home _____ Work _____

Cell _____ Email _____

G

Every breath of air and ray of light and heat, every beautiful prospect, is, as it were, the skirt of their garment, the waving of the robes of those whose faces see God.

— John Henry Newman

G

Name

Address

Home   Work

Cell   Email

Name

Address

Home   Work

Cell   Email

Name

Address

Home   Work

Cell   Email

Name

Address

Home   Work

Cell   Email

Name

Address

Home   Work

Cell   Email

Every visible thing in this world is put in the charge of an Angel.

— St. Augustine

Name _____

Address _____

_____

Home _____ Work _____

Cell _____ Email _____

Name _____

Address _____

_____

Home _____ Work _____

Cell _____ Email _____

Name _____

Address _____

_____

Home _____ Work _____

Cell _____ Email _____

Name _____

Address _____

_____

Home _____ Work _____

Cell _____ Email _____

G

G

Name _____

Address _____

_____

Home _____ Work _____

Cell _____ Email _____

Name _____

Address _____

_____

Home _____ Work _____

Cell _____ Email _____

Name _____

Address _____

_____

Home _____ Work _____

Cell _____ Email _____

Name _____

Address _____

_____

Home _____ Work _____

Cell _____ Email _____

Name _____

Address _____

_____

Home _____ Work _____

Cell _____ Email _____

Name _____

Address _____

_____

Home _____ Work _____

Cell _____ Email _____

Name _____

Address _____

_____

Home _____ Work _____

Cell _____ Email _____

Name _____

Address _____

_____

Home _____ Work _____

Cell _____ Email _____

Name _____

Address _____

_____

Home _____ Work _____

Cell _____ Email _____

H

Perhaps children's innocence, wherever it comes from, contributes to the fact that they seem to see angels more often.

— John Ronner

H

Name _____

Address _____

_____

Home _____ Work _____

Cell _____ Email _____

Name _____

Address _____

_____

Home _____ Work _____

Cell _____ Email _____

Name _____

Address _____

_____

Home _____ Work _____

Cell _____ Email _____

Name _____

Address _____

_____

Home _____ Work _____

Cell _____ Email _____

Name _____

Address _____

_____

Home _____ Work _____

Cell _____ Email _____

The angel ended, and in Adam's ear
So charming left his voice that he awhile
thought him still speaking, still stood fix'd to hear.

– John Milton

Name _____

Address _____

_____

Home _____ Work _____

Cell _____ Email _____

Name _____

Address _____

_____

Home _____ Work _____

Cell _____ Email _____

Name _____

Address _____

_____

Home _____ Work _____

Cell _____ Email _____

Name _____

Address _____

_____

Home _____ Work _____

Cell _____ Email _____

H

Name _____

Address _____

_____

Home _____ Work _____

Cell _____ Email _____

Name _____

Address _____

_____

Home _____ Work _____

Cell _____ Email _____

Name _____

Address _____

_____

Home _____ Work _____

Cell _____ Email _____

Name _____

Address _____

_____

Home _____ Work _____

Cell _____ Email _____

Name _____

Address _____

_____

Home _____ Work _____

Cell _____ Email _____

Name _____

Address _____

_____

Home _____ Work _____

Cell _____ Email _____

Name _____

Address _____

_____

Home _____ Work _____

Cell _____ Email _____

Name _____

Address _____

_____

Home _____ Work _____

Cell _____ Email _____

Name _____

Address _____

_____

Home _____ Work _____

Cell _____ Email _____

An angel can illuminate the thought and mind of man by strengthening the power of vision, and by bringing within his reach some truth which the angel himself contemplates.

– St. Thomas Aquinas

Name _____

Address _____

_____

Home _____ Work _____

Cell _____ Email _____

Name _____

Address _____

_____

Home _____ Work _____

Cell _____ Email _____

Name _____

Address _____

_____

Home _____ Work _____

Cell _____ Email _____

Name _____

Address _____

_____

Home _____ Work _____

Cell _____ Email _____

Name _____

Address _____

_____

Home _____ Work _____

Cell _____ Email _____

For the tear is an intellectual thing,
And a sigh is the sword of an Angel
King.

— *William Blake*

Name _____

Address _____

_____

Home _____ Work _____

Cell _____ Email _____

Name _____

Address _____

_____

Home _____ Work _____

Cell _____ Email _____

Name _____

Address _____

_____

Home _____ Work _____

Cell _____ Email _____

Name _____

Address _____

_____

Home _____ Work _____

Cell _____ Email _____

Name _____

Address _____

_____

Home _____ Work _____

Cell _____ Email _____

Name _____

Address _____

_____

Home _____ Work _____

Cell _____ Email _____

Name _____

Address _____

_____

Home _____ Work _____

Cell _____ Email _____

Name _____

Address _____

_____

Home _____ Work _____

Cell _____ Email _____

Name _____

Address _____

_____

Home _____ Work _____

Cell _____ Email _____

Name _____

Address _____

_____

Home _____ Work _____

Cell _____ Email _____

Name _____

Address _____

_____

Home _____ Work _____

Cell _____ Email _____

Name _____

Address _____

_____

Home _____ Work _____

Cell _____ Email _____

Name _____

Address _____

_____

Home _____ Work _____

Cell _____ Email _____

There is, therefore, a more perfect intellectual life in the Angels. In them the intellect does not proceed to self-knowledge from anything exterior, but knows itself through itself.

— St. Thomas Aquinas

Name

Address

Home   Work

Cell   Email

Name

Address

Home   Work

Cell   Email

Name

Address

Home   Work

Cell   Email

Name

Address

Home   Work

Cell   Email

Name

Address

Home   Work

Cell   Email

Name _____

Address _____

_____

Home _____ Work _____

Cell _____ Email _____

Name _____

Address _____

_____

Home _____ Work _____

Cell _____ Email _____

Name _____

Address _____

_____

Home _____ Work _____

Cell _____ Email _____

Name _____

Address _____

_____

Home _____ Work _____

Cell _____ Email _____

J

Angels are unsatisfiable in their longing to do by all means all manner of good unto all the creatures… especially the children of men.

— Richard Hooker

Name _____

Address _____

_____

Home _____ Work _____

Cell _____ Email _____

Name _____

Address _____

_____

Home _____ Work _____

Cell _____ Email _____

Name _____

Address _____

_____

Home _____ Work _____

Cell _____ Email _____

Name _____

Address _____

_____

Home _____ Work _____

Cell _____ Email _____

Name _____

Address _____

_____

Home _____ Work _____

Cell _____ Email _____

Keep your good deeds for others a secret, just as your Angel works behind the scenes in your own life.

— *Eileen Elias Freeman*

Name _____

Address _____

_____

Home _____ Work _____

Cell _____ Email _____

Name _____

Address _____

_____

Home _____ Work _____

Cell _____ Email _____

Name _____

Address _____

_____

Home _____ Work _____

Cell _____ Email _____

J

Name _____

Address _____

_____

Home _____ Work _____

Cell _____ Email _____

Name _____

Address _____

_____

Home _____ Work _____

Cell _____ Email _____

Name _____

Address _____

_____

Home _____ Work _____

Cell _____ Email _____

Name _____

Address _____

_____

Home _____ Work _____

Cell _____ Email _____

Name _____

Address _____

_____

Home _____ Work _____

Cell _____ Email _____

Name _____

Address _____

_____

Home _____ Work _____

Cell _____ Email _____

Name _____

Address _____

_____

Home _____ Work _____

Cell _____ Email _____

Name _____

Address _____

_____

Home _____ Work _____

Cell _____ Email _____

Name _____

Address _____

_____

Home _____ Work _____

Cell _____ Email _____

Name _____

Address _____

_____

Home _____ Work _____

Cell _____ Email _____

It is not because angels are holier than men or devils that makes them angels,
but because they do not expect holiness from one another, but from God alone.
— William Blake

Name _____

Address _____

_____

Home _____ Work _____

Cell _____ Email _____

Name _____

Address _____

_____

Home _____ Work _____

Cell _____ Email _____

Name _____

Address _____

_____

Home _____ Work _____

Cell _____ Email _____

Name _____

Address _____

_____

Home _____ Work _____

Cell _____ Email _____

Name _____

Address _____

_____

Home _____ Work _____

Cell _____ Email _____

We sell the thrones of angels for a short and turbulent pleasure.

— *Ralph Waldo Emerson*

Name _____

Address _____

_____

Home _____ Work _____

Cell _____ Email _____

Name _____

Address _____

_____

Home _____ Work _____

Cell _____ Email _____

Name _____

Address _____

_____

Home _____ Work _____

Cell _____ Email _____

Name _____

Address _____

_____

Home _____ Work _____

Cell _____ Email _____

Name _____

Address _____

_____

Home _____ Work _____

Cell _____ Email _____

Name _____

Address _____

_____

Home _____ Work _____

Cell _____ Email _____

Name _____

Address _____

_____

Home _____ Work _____

Cell _____ Email _____

Name _____

Address _____

_____

Home _____ Work _____

Cell _____ Email _____

Name _____

Address _____

_____

Home _____ Work _____

Cell _____ Email _____

Name _____

Address _____

_____

Home _____ Work _____

Cell _____ Email _____

Name _____

Address _____

_____

Home _____ Work _____

Cell _____ Email _____

Name _____

Address _____

_____

Home _____ Work _____

Cell _____ Email _____

Name _____

Address _____

_____

Home _____ Work _____

Cell _____ Email _____

The Angel that presided o'er my birth
Said, Little creature, formed of joy and mirth,
Go love without the help of anything on earth.

— William Blake

Name

Address

Home   Work

Cell   Email

Name

Address

Home   Work

Cell   Email

Name

Address

Home   Work

Cell   Email

Name

Address

Home   Work

Cell   Email

Name

Address

Home   Work

Cell   Email

Every man contemplates an angel in his future self.
— Ralph Waldo Emerson

Name _____

Address _____

_____

Home _____ Work _____

Cell _____ Email _____

Name _____

Address _____

_____

Home _____ Work _____

Cell _____ Email _____

Name _____

Address _____

_____

Home _____ Work _____

Cell _____ Email _____

Name _____

Address _____

_____

Home _____ Work _____

Cell _____ Email _____

Name _____

Address _____

_____

Home _____ Work _____

Cell _____ Email _____

Name _____

Address _____

_____

Home _____ Work _____

Cell _____ Email _____

Name _____

Address _____

_____

Home _____ Work _____

Cell _____ Email _____

Name _____

Address _____

_____

Home _____ Work _____

Cell _____ Email _____

Name _____

Address _____

_____

Home _____ Work _____

Cell _____ Email _____

To see the angel in the malady requires an eye for the invisible, a certain blinding of one eye and an opening of the other to elsewhere.

— James Hillman

Name _____

Address _____

_____

Home _____ Work _____

Cell _____ Email _____

Name _____

Address _____

_____

Home _____ Work _____

Cell _____ Email _____

Name _____

Address _____

_____

Home _____ Work _____

Cell _____ Email _____

Name _____

Address _____

_____

Home _____ Work _____

Cell _____ Email _____

Name _____

Address _____

_____

Home _____ Work _____

Cell _____ Email _____

Name _____

Address _____

_____

Home _____ Work _____

Cell _____ Email _____

Name _____

Address _____

_____

Home _____ Work _____

Cell _____ Email _____

Name _____

Address _____

_____

Home _____ Work _____

Cell _____ Email _____

Name _____

Address _____

_____

Home _____ Work _____

Cell _____ Email _____

Name _____

Address _____

_____

Home _____ Work _____

Cell _____ Email _____

Name _____

Address _____

_____

Home _____ Work _____

Cell _____ Email _____

Name _____

Address _____

_____

Home _____ Work _____

Cell _____ Email _____

Name _____

Address _____

_____

Home _____ Work _____

Cell _____ Email _____

*A person is disposed to an act of choice by an angel in two ways. Sometimes,
a man's understanding is enlightened by an angel to know what is good, but it
is not instructed as to the reason why. But sometimes he is instructed by angelic
illumination, both that this act is good and as to the reason why it is good.*

— St. Thomas Aquinas

Name _____

Address _____

_____

Home _____ Work _____

Cell _____ Email _____

Name _____

Address _____

_____

Home _____ Work _____

Cell _____ Email _____

Name _____

Address _____

_____

Home _____ Work _____

Cell _____ Email _____

Name _____

Address _____

_____

Home _____ Work _____

Cell _____ Email _____

Name _____

Address _____

_____

Home _____ Work _____

Cell _____ Email _____

Name _____

Address _____

_____

Home _____ Work _____

Cell _____ Email _____

Name _____

Address _____

_____

Home _____ Work _____

Cell _____ Email _____

Name _____

Address _____

_____

Home _____ Work _____

Cell _____ Email _____

Name _____

Address _____

_____

Home _____ Work _____

Cell _____ Email _____

Angels may live in the celestial gardens of heaven but they work in the formidable landscape of the human heart.

— *Georges Luis Guevara*

N

Name _____

Address _____

_____

Home _____ Work _____

Cell _____ Email _____

Name _____

Address _____

_____

Home _____ Work _____

Cell _____ Email _____

Name _____

Address _____

_____

Home _____ Work _____

Cell _____ Email _____

Name _____

Address _____

_____

Home _____ Work _____

Cell _____ Email _____

Name _____

Address _____

_____

Home _____ Work _____

Cell _____ Email _____

Man is neither angel or beast; and the misfortune is that he who would act the angel acts the beast.

— *Blaise Pascal*

Name _____

Address _____

_____

Home _____ Work _____

Cell _____ Email _____

Name _____

Address _____

_____

Home _____ Work _____

Cell _____ Email _____

Name _____

Address _____

_____

Home _____ Work _____

Cell _____ Email _____

Name _____

Address _____

_____

Home _____ Work _____

Cell _____ Email _____

O

Name _____

Address _____

_____

Home _____ Work _____

Cell _____ Email _____

Name _____

Address _____

_____

Home _____ Work _____

Cell _____ Email _____

Name _____

Address _____

_____

Home _____ Work _____

Cell _____ Email _____

Name _____

Address _____

_____

Home _____ Work _____

Cell _____ Email _____

Name _____

Address _____

_____

Home _____ Work _____

Cell _____ Email _____

Name _____

Address _____

_____

Home _____ Work _____

Cell _____ Email _____

Name _____

Address _____

_____

Home _____ Work _____

Cell _____ Email _____

Name _____

Address _____

_____

Home _____ Work _____

Cell _____ Email _____

Name _____

Address _____

_____

Home _____ Work _____

Cell _____ Email _____

I saw Gabriel, like a maiden, or like the moon amongst the stars. His hair was like a woman's, falling in long tresses... He is the most beautiful of Angels.

— Ruzbehan Baqli

O

Name _____

Address _____

_____

Home _____ Work _____

Cell _____ Email _____

Name _____

Address _____

_____

Home _____ Work _____

Cell _____ Email _____

Name _____

Address _____

_____

Home _____ Work _____

Cell _____ Email _____

Name _____

Address _____

_____

Home _____ Work _____

Cell _____ Email _____

Name _____

Address _____

_____

Home _____ Work _____

Cell _____ Email _____

To those who are willing to believe, no explanation of these events is necessary. And to those who are not willing to believe, no explanation is possible.

— Joan Wester Anderson

Name _____

Address _____

_____

Home _____ Work _____

Cell _____ Email _____

Name _____

Address _____

_____

Home _____ Work _____

Cell _____ Email _____

Name _____

Address _____

_____

Home _____ Work _____

Cell _____ Email _____

Name _____

Address _____

_____

Home _____ Work _____

Cell _____ Email _____

O

Name _____

Address _____

_____

Home _____ Work _____

Cell _____ Email _____

Name _____

Address _____

_____

Home _____ Work _____

Cell _____ Email _____

Name _____

Address _____

_____

Home _____ Work _____

Cell _____ Email _____

Name _____

Address _____

_____

Home _____ Work _____

Cell _____ Email _____

Name _____

Address _____

_____

Home _____ Work _____

Cell _____ Email _____

Name _____

Address _____

_____

Home _____ Work _____

Cell _____ Email _____

Name _____

Address _____

_____

Home _____ Work _____

Cell _____ Email _____

Name _____

Address _____

_____

Home _____ Work _____

Cell _____ Email _____

Name _____

Address _____

_____

Home _____ Work _____

Cell _____ Email _____

O, what may man within him hide,
Though angel on the outward side!
— William Shakespeare

Name _____

Address _____

_____

Home _____ Work _____

Cell _____ Email _____

Name _____

Address _____

_____

Home _____ Work _____

Cell _____ Email _____

Name _____

Address _____

_____

Home _____ Work _____

Cell _____ Email _____

Name _____

Address _____

_____

Home _____ Work _____

Cell _____ Email _____

Name _____

Address _____

_____

Home _____ Work _____

Cell _____ Email _____

Millions of spiritual creatures walk the earth unseen,
both when we wake and when we sleep.

– John Milton

Name _____

Address _____

_____

Home _____ Work _____

Cell _____ Email _____

Name _____

Address _____

_____

Home _____ Work _____

Cell _____ Email _____

Name _____

Address _____

_____

Home _____ Work _____

Cell _____ Email _____

Name _____

Address _____

_____

Home _____ Work _____

Cell _____ Email _____

Name _____

Address _____

_____

Home _____ Work _____

Cell _____ Email _____

Name _____

Address _____

_____

Home _____ Work _____

Cell _____ Email _____

Name _____

Address _____

_____

Home _____ Work _____

Cell _____ Email _____

Name _____

Address _____

_____

Home _____ Work _____

Cell _____ Email _____

Name _____

Address _____

_____

Home _____ Work _____

Cell _____ Email _____

Name _____

Address _____

_____

Home _____ Work _____

Cell _____ Email _____

Name _____

Address _____

_____

Home _____ Work _____

Cell _____ Email _____

Name _____

Address _____

_____

Home _____ Work _____

Cell _____ Email _____

Name _____

Address _____

_____

Home _____ Work _____

Cell _____ Email _____

If instead of a gem, or even a flower, we should cast the gift of a loving
thought into the heart of a friend, that would be giving as the angels give.

— George MacDonald

Q

Name _____

Address _____

_____

Home _____ Work _____

Cell _____ Email _____

Name _____

Address _____

_____

Home _____ Work _____

Cell _____ Email _____

Name _____

Address _____

_____

Home _____ Work _____

Cell _____ Email _____

Name _____

Address _____

_____

Home _____ Work _____

Cell _____ Email _____

Name _____

Address _____

_____

Home _____ Work _____

Cell _____ Email _____

A man does not have to be an Angel in order to be a saint.

— Albert Schweitzer

Q

Name _____

Address _____

_____

Home _____ Work _____

Cell _____ Email _____

Name _____

Address _____

_____

Home _____ Work _____

Cell _____ Email _____

Name _____

Address _____

_____

Home _____ Work _____

Cell _____ Email _____

Name _____

Address _____

_____

Home _____ Work _____

Cell _____ Email _____

Q

Name _____

Address _____

_____

Home _____ Work _____

Cell _____ Email _____

Name _____

Address _____

_____

Home _____ Work _____

Cell _____ Email _____

Name _____

Address _____

_____

Home _____ Work _____

Cell _____ Email _____

Name _____

Address _____

_____

Home _____ Work _____

Cell _____ Email _____

Name _____

Address _____

_____

Home _____ Work _____

Cell _____ Email _____

Name _____

Address _____

_____

Home _____ Work _____

Cell _____ Email _____

Name _____

Address _____

_____

Home _____ Work _____

Cell _____ Email _____

Name _____

Address _____

_____

Home _____ Work _____

Cell _____ Email _____

Name _____

Address _____

_____

Home _____ Work _____

Cell _____ Email _____

I want to be an angel,
And with the angels stand
A crown upon my forehead
A harp within my hand.
– Urania Locke Bailey

R

Name _____

Address _____

_____

Home _____ Work _____

Cell _____ Email _____

Name _____

Address _____

_____

Home _____ Work _____

Cell _____ Email _____

Name _____

Address _____

_____

Home _____ Work _____

Cell _____ Email _____

Name _____

Address _____

_____

Home _____ Work _____

Cell _____ Email _____

Name _____

Address _____

_____

Home _____ Work _____

Cell _____ Email _____

It is only with the heart that one can see rightly; what is essential is invisible to the eye.

— *Antoine De Saint-Exupery*

Name _____

Address _____

_____

Home _____ Work _____

Cell _____ Email _____

Name _____

Address _____

_____

Home _____ Work _____

Cell _____ Email _____

Name _____

Address _____

_____

Home _____ Work _____

Cell _____ Email _____

Name _____

Address _____

_____

Home _____ Work _____

Cell _____ Email _____

R

Name _____

Address _____

_____

Home _____ Work _____

Cell _____ Email _____

Name _____

Address _____

_____

Home _____ Work _____

Cell _____ Email _____

Name _____

Address _____

_____

Home _____ Work _____

Cell _____ Email _____

Name _____

Address _____

_____

Home _____ Work _____

Cell _____ Email _____

Name _____

Address _____

_____

Home _____ Work _____

Cell _____ Email _____

Name _____

Address _____

_____

Home _____ Work _____

Cell _____ Email _____

Name _____

Address _____

_____

Home _____ Work _____

Cell _____ Email _____

Name _____

Address _____

_____

Home _____ Work _____

Cell _____ Email _____

Name _____

Address _____

_____

Home _____ Work _____

Cell _____ Email _____

Sleep my child, and peace attend thee
All through the night.
Guardian angels God will send thee,
All through the night.

— Sir Harold Boulton

Name _____

Address _____

_____

Home _____ Work _____

Cell _____ Email _____

Name _____

Address _____

_____

Home _____ Work _____

Cell _____ Email _____

Name _____

Address _____

_____

Home _____ Work _____

Cell _____ Email _____

Name _____

Address _____

_____

Home _____ Work _____

Cell _____ Email _____

Name _____

Address _____

_____

Home _____ Work _____

Cell _____ Email _____

S

The Angels come to visit us, and we only know them when they are gone.

— George Eliot

Name _____

Address _____

_____

Home _____ Work _____

Cell _____ Email _____

Name _____

Address _____

_____

Home _____ Work _____

Cell _____ Email _____

Name _____

Address _____

_____

Home _____ Work _____

Cell _____ Email _____

Name _____

Address _____

_____

Home _____ Work _____

Cell _____ Email _____

S

S

Name _____

Address _____

_____

Home _____ Work _____

Cell _____ Email _____

Name _____

Address _____

_____

Home _____ Work _____

Cell _____ Email _____

Name _____

Address _____

_____

Home _____ Work _____

Cell _____ Email _____

Name _____

Address _____

_____

Home _____ Work _____

Cell _____ Email _____

Name _____

Address _____

_____

Home _____ Work _____

Cell _____ Email _____

Name _____

Address _____

_____

Home _____ Work _____

Cell _____ Email _____

Name _____

Address _____

_____

Home _____ Work _____

Cell _____ Email _____

Name _____

Address _____

_____

Home _____ Work _____

Cell _____ Email _____

Name _____

Address _____

_____

Home _____ Work _____

Cell _____ Email _____

Silently one by one, in the infinite meadows of heaven
Blossomed the lovely stars, the forget-me-nots, of angels.
– Henry Wadsworth Longfellow

S

Name _____

Address _____

_____

Home _____ Work _____

Cell _____ Email _____

Name _____

Address _____

_____

Home _____ Work _____

Cell _____ Email _____

S

Name _____

Address _____

_____

Home _____ Work _____

Cell _____ Email _____

Name _____

Address _____

_____

Home _____ Work _____

Cell _____ Email _____

Name _____

Address _____

_____

Home _____ Work _____

Cell _____ Email _____

May I burst with jubilant praise to assenting Angels.

— Rainer Maria Rilke

Name _____

Address _____

_____

Home _____ Work _____

Cell _____ Email _____

Name _____

Address _____

_____

Home _____ Work _____

Cell _____ Email _____

Name _____

Address _____

_____

Home _____ Work _____

Cell _____ Email _____

Name _____

Address _____

_____

Home _____ Work _____

Cell _____ Email _____

Name _____

Address _____

_____

Home _____ Work _____

Cell _____ Email _____

Name _____

Address _____

_____

Home _____ Work _____

Cell _____ Email _____

Name _____

Address _____

_____

Home _____ Work _____

Cell _____ Email _____

Name _____

Address _____

_____

Home _____ Work _____

Cell _____ Email _____

Name _____

Address _____

_____

Home _____ Work _____

Cell _____ Email _____

T

Name _____

Address _____

_____

Home _____ Work _____

Cell _____ Email _____

Name _____

Address _____

_____

Home _____ Work _____

Cell _____ Email _____

Name _____

Address _____

_____

Home _____ Work _____

Cell _____ Email _____

T

Name _____

Address _____

_____

Home _____ Work _____

Cell _____ Email _____

Stone walls do not a prison make,
Nor iron bars a cage;
Minds innocent of quiet take
That for an hermitage;
If I have freedom in my love
And in my soul am free,
Angels alone that soar above
Enjoy such liberty.   *— Richard Lovelace*

Name _____

Address _____

_____

Home _____ Work _____

Cell _____ Email _____

Name _____

Address _____

_____

Home _____ Work _____

Cell _____ Email _____

Name _____

Address _____

_____

Home _____ Work _____

Cell _____ Email _____

Name _____

Address _____

_____

Home _____ Work _____

Cell _____ Email _____

Name _____

Address _____

_____

Home _____ Work _____

Cell _____ Email _____

And the Angel said, "I have learned that every man lives, not through care of himself, but by love."

— Leo Tolstoy

Name _____

Address _____

_____

Home _____ Work _____

Cell _____ Email _____

Name _____

Address _____

_____

Home _____ Work _____

Cell _____ Email _____

Name _____

Address _____

_____

Home _____ Work _____

Cell _____ Email _____

Name _____

Address _____

_____

Home _____ Work _____

Cell _____ Email _____

T

U

Name _____

Address _____

_____

Home _____ Work _____

Cell _____ Email _____

Name _____

Address _____

_____

Home _____ Work _____

Cell _____ Email _____

Name _____

Address _____

_____

Home _____ Work _____

Cell _____ Email _____

Name _____

Address _____

_____

Home _____ Work _____

Cell _____ Email _____

Name _____

Address _____

_____

Home _____ Work _____

Cell _____ Email _____

Name _____

Address _____

_____

Home _____ Work _____

Cell _____ Email _____

Name _____

Address _____

_____

Home _____ Work _____

Cell _____ Email _____

Name _____

Address _____

_____

Home _____ Work _____

Cell _____ Email _____

Name _____

Address _____

_____

Home _____ Work _____

Cell _____ Email _____

The more materialistic science becomes, the more angels I shall paint. Their wings are my protest in favor of the immortality of the soul.

— Edward Burne-Jones

U

Name _____

Address _____

_____

Home _____ Work _____

Cell _____ Email _____

Name _____

Address _____

_____

Home _____ Work _____

Cell _____ Email _____

Name _____

Address _____

_____

Home _____ Work _____

Cell _____ Email _____

Name _____

Address _____

_____

Home _____ Work _____

Cell _____ Email _____

Name _____

Address _____

_____

Home _____ Work _____

Cell _____ Email _____

I am the Angel of the Sun
Whose flaming wheels began to run
When God's almighty breath
Said to the darkness and the Night,
Let there be light! and there was light.
— Henry Wadsworth Longfellow

Name _____

Address _____

_____

Home _____ Work _____

Cell _____ Email _____

Name _____

Address _____

_____

Home _____ Work _____

Cell _____ Email _____

Name _____

Address _____

_____

Home _____ Work _____

Cell _____ Email _____

Name _____

Address _____

_____

Home _____ Work _____

Cell _____ Email _____

V

Name _____

Address _____

_____

Home _____ Work _____

Cell _____ Email _____

Name _____

Address _____

_____

Home _____ Work _____

Cell _____ Email _____

Name _____

Address _____

_____

Home _____ Work _____

Cell _____ Email _____

V

Name _____

Address _____

_____

Home _____ Work _____

Cell _____ Email _____

Name _____

Address _____

_____

Home _____ Work _____

Cell _____ Email _____

Name _____

Address _____

_____

Home _____ Work _____

Cell _____ Email _____

Name _____

Address _____

_____

Home _____ Work _____

Cell _____ Email _____

Name _____

Address _____

_____

Home _____ Work _____

Cell _____ Email _____

Name _____

Address _____

_____

Home _____ Work _____

Cell _____ Email _____

V

Think, In mountain higher,
The angels would press on us, and aspire
To drop some golden orb of perfect song
Into our deep, dear silence.

— Elizabeth Barrett Browning

Name

Address

Home   Work

Cell   Email

Name

Address

Home   Work

Cell   Email

Name

Address

Home   Work

Cell   Email

Name

Address

Home   Work

Cell   Email

W

Name

Address

Home   Work

Cell   Email

To love for the sake of being loved is human, but to love for the sake of loving is angelic.

— *Alphonse de Lamartine*

Name _____

Address _____

_____

Home _____ Work _____

Cell _____ Email _____

Name _____

Address _____

_____

Home _____ Work _____

Cell _____ Email _____

Name _____

Address _____

_____

Home _____ Work _____

Cell _____ Email _____

Name _____

Address _____

_____

Home _____ Work _____

Cell _____ Email _____

Name

Address

Home   Work

Cell   Email

Name

Address

Home   Work

Cell   Email

Name

Address

Home   Work

Cell   Email

Name

Address

Home   Work

Cell   Email

Name

Address

Home   Work

Cell   Email

W

Name _____

Address _____

_____

Home _____ Work _____

Cell _____ Email _____

Name _____

Address _____

_____

Home _____ Work _____

Cell _____ Email _____

Name _____

Address _____

_____

Home _____ Work _____

Cell _____ Email _____

Name _____

Address _____

_____

Home _____ Work _____

Cell _____ Email _____

Make yourself familiar with the angels, and behold them frequently in spirit;
for without being seen, they are present with you.

— Saint Francis de Sales

Name _____

Address _____

_____

Home _____ Work _____

Cell _____ Email _____

Name _____

Address _____

_____

Home _____ Work _____

Cell _____ Email _____

Name _____

Address _____

_____

Home _____ Work _____

Cell _____ Email _____

Name _____

Address _____

_____

Home _____ Work _____

Cell _____ Email _____

Name _____

Address _____

_____

Home _____ Work _____

Cell _____ Email _____

W

Perhaps one day there will be a time when we can all share the capacity for joy that angels have frolicking in the fields of innocence and swimming in the glorious colours of the universe.
— *Georges Luis Guevara*

Name _____

Address _____

_____

Home _____ Work _____

Cell _____ Email _____

Name _____

Address _____

_____

Home _____ Work _____

Cell _____ Email _____

Name _____

Address _____

_____

Home _____ Work _____

Cell _____ Email _____

Name _____

Address _____

_____

Home _____ Work _____

Cell _____ Email _____

Name _____

Address _____

_____

Home _____ Work _____

Cell _____ Email _____

Name _____

Address _____

_____

Home _____ Work _____

Cell _____ Email _____

Name _____

Address _____

_____

Home _____ Work _____

Cell _____ Email _____

Name _____

Address _____

_____

Home _____ Work _____

Cell _____ Email _____

X

Name _____

Address _____

_____

Home _____ Work _____

Cell _____ Email _____

Name _____

Address _____

_____

Home _____ Work _____

Cell _____ Email _____

Name _____

Address _____

_____

Home _____ Work _____

Cell _____ Email _____

Name _____

Address _____

_____

Home _____ Work _____

Cell _____ Email _____

Name _____

Address _____

_____

Home _____ Work _____

Cell _____ Email _____

We can all be angels to one another. We can choose to obey the still small stirring within, the little whispers that says, Go. Ask. Reach out. Be an answer to someone's plea. You have a part to play. Have faith.

— Joan Wester Anderson

Name _____

Address _____

_____

Home _____ Work _____

Cell _____ Email _____

Name _____

Address _____

_____

Home _____ Work _____

Cell _____ Email _____

Name _____

Address _____

_____

Home _____ Work _____

Cell _____ Email _____

Name _____

Address _____

_____

Home _____ Work _____

Cell _____ Email _____

Name _____

Address _____

_____

Home _____ Work _____

Cell _____ Email _____

Angels have always inspired us. They reside in our hearts and minds somewhere between our conviction for faith and our need to believe.

— *Georges Luis Guevara*

Name _____

Address _____

_____

Home _____ Work _____

Cell _____ Email _____

Name _____

Address _____

_____

Home _____ Work _____

Cell _____ Email _____

Name _____

Address _____

_____

Home _____ Work _____

Cell _____ Email _____

Name _____

Address _____

_____

Home _____ Work _____

Cell _____ Email _____

Name _____

Address _____

_____

Home _____ Work _____

Cell _____ Email _____

Name _____

Address _____

_____

Home _____ Work _____

Cell _____ Email _____

Name _____

Address _____

_____

Home _____ Work _____

Cell _____ Email _____

Name _____

Address _____

_____

Home _____ Work _____

Cell _____ Email _____

Name _____

Address _____

_____

Home _____ Work _____

Cell _____ Email _____

ST. FILIPP: METROPOLITAN OF MOSCOW—
Encounter with Ivan the Terrible

VOLUME ONE
IN THE COLLECTED WORKS OF
GEORGE P. FEDOTOV

ST. FILIPP METROPOLITAN OF MOSCOW –

Encounter with Ivan the Terrible

BY GEORGE P. FEDOTOV

Translated from Russian by
Richard Haugh and Nickolas Lupinin

VOLUME ONE
in *The Collected Works* of
George P. Fedotov

EDITOR: Richard Haugh
ASSOCIATE EDITORS: Nickolas Lupinin and Michael Meerson-Aksenov

NORDLAND PUBLISHING COMPANY
Belmont, Massachusetts 02178
1978

BY THE SAME AUTHOR

The Collected Works of George P. Fedotov
[NORDLAND Publishing Company]

First published in Russian by YMCA Press in 1928
as *Sviatoi Filipp: Mitropolit Moskovskii*
Library of Congress Catalog Card Number 75-27-477
ISBN 0-913124-14-1
© Copyright 1978 by Nina Rojankovsky
Administratrix of the Estate of George P. Fedotov

GEORGE P. FEDOTOV

ABOUT THE AUTHOR

George P. Fedotov was born in 1886 in Saratov, Russia. He began his academic life as a student of engineering but, while studying in Germany and Italy, he changed his scope of study to history. When he returned to Russia in 1914, he became Assistant Professor of European Medieval History at the University of St. Petersburg (1914-1918) and, later, Professor at the University of Saratov (1920-1922). Unable to pursue creative scholarship in Soviet Russia, Professor Fedotov left his homeland in 1925. From 1926 to 1940 he was Professor of Church History at the Russian Theological School in Paris. During this time in Paris he also worked on the journals *Sovremennyi zapiski* [*Contemporary Votes*], *Put'* [*The Way*] and *Chisla* [*Dates*]. In 1931 he co-founded the important journal *Novyi Grad* [*The New City*] which he edited until 1939. In 1941 he came to the United States where, until his death in 1951, he was Professor of Church History at St. Vladimir's Theological School.

ABOUT *THE COLLECTED WORKS* OF
GEORGE P. FEDOTOV

George P. Fedotov wrote prolifically and his interests ranged over several fields of inquiry—Russian history, literature, theology, spirituality and Russian culture in general as well as political thought and the Latin West. *The Collected Works of George P. Fedotov* will be published in English and will include his numerous articles as well as his books—including reprints of those books which were already published in English. Volumes I–IV are presently available.

Vol. II– *A Treasury of Russian Spirituality* (paper) 501 pp.
Vol. III– *The Russian Religious Mind (I): Kievan Christianity—The 10th-13th Centuries* 431 pp.
Vol. IV– *The Russian Religious Mind (II): The Middle Ages—The 13th-15th Centuries* 405 pp.
Vol. V– *Peter Abelard*

[Other volumes forthcoming]

ABOUT THE EDITORS

Richard Haugh
Editor

Dr. Richard Haugh, recipient of numerous honors, was a National Endowment for the Humanities' 'Fellow in Residence' in Medieval Studies at Harvard University (1976-1977), was invited to be a Visiting Scholar at Harvard Divinity School, was awarded a Mellon Fellowship in Humanities at Emory University, and invited to be Visiting Professor of Religious Studies at Rice University. Dr. Haugh, Associate Professor of Humanities at Tuskegee Institute, is the author of articles in the disciplines of religion, history and literature. Translator of religious and philosophical essays and works from German, French, Latin and Greek, Dr. Haugh is editor of *The Collected Works of George P. Fedotov*, editor-in-chief of *Ways of Russian Theology* by Georges Florovsky, and an editor of the journal *Transactions*. He has authored *Photius and the Carolingians* and is co-editor of and contributor to *Aleksandr Solzhenitsyn: Critical Essays and Documentary Materials*. He is presently completing a major work on 8th-century comparative Latin and Byzantine religious and intellectual history, as well as working on a book on Augustine and John Cassian. He is the founder, and chairman of the board of trustees, of Falmouth Academy.

Nickolas Lupinin
Associate Editor

Dr. Nickolas Lupinin, whose reviews, articles and translations have appeared—*inter alia*—in *Russian Review, Transactions* and *Church History*, is Associate Editor of *The Collected Works of George P. Fedotov*, translator and editor of *Russian Historiography* by George Vernadsky and *Catherine the Great Takes Power* by S. M. Soloviev. Dr. Lupinin is the author of a forthcoming book entitled *Russia in Turmoil: Church, Schism and State in the 17th Century*. He is presently completing a social history of Russia in the 17th century. Dr. Lupinin is also a specialist in the history and culture of the Middle East.

Michael Meerson-Aksenov
Associate Editor

Michael Meerson-Aksenov is a religious philosopher and a socio-political *samizdat* writer. After a lengthy spiritual evolution he converted to Christianity in 1966. He taught for a short time at one of Moscow's special schools, but was asked to leave because his conception of Russian social thought did not correspond to the one which was officially accepted. His most important *samizdat* work is *The Two Testaments: Toward a Jewish-Christian Dialogue in Russia* (1972). With the increase in the repression of dissidents toward the end of 1972 he emigrated from the USSR.

CONTENTS

INTRODUCTION

The Russian Church has been frequently berated for neglecting the social problems of Christian culture. From time to time, even from within the Russian Church, there are voices asserting the exclusivity of the personal way, of the individual feat and of personal salvation. Every statement of social goals for the Orthodox Church is rejected as a Roman Catholic temptation which, in being rejected, leads to an original brand of ascetical Protestantism: the heavenly kingdom and Caesar's kingdom are forever separate. This spiritual and metaphysical division does not interfere with the blessing of Caesar's kingdom which then means, precisely because of religious renunciation, that this blessing has no limit. Every authority, and every act of this authority, is blessed. The question of *justice* is not raised. Such an issue, it is felt, belongs to the internal domain of the Church. Submissiveness to unjust rule may even be preached as an ascetical exploit.

For the historian it is clear that in these broadly diffused attitudes we are confronted with the ascetical tradition of the ancient Christian East and the results, Protestant in tendency, of Tsar Peter's Church reform. For a long time Peter's reform distorted the socio-national image of Russian Orthodoxy, leaving its inner spiritual life inviolable. The saintly elder [*starets*] and the submissive hierarch became the two poles of Church life.

Such was not always the case. In ancient Russia relations between Church and State were different. Of course, the Orthodox Church — and here is its great advantage over the Western Church — never reached out for power, never grabbed for Caesar's sword. But, because of the essential intertwining of all social and ecclesiastical life, the Church was drawn into worldly affairs. Its un-imperious though authoritative voice was consulted in every important governmental matter. The Tsar sought advice not only from his boyars but also from his father and *Bogomolets* — the Metropolitan or Patriarch. The "Holy Council" ["*Osviashchennyi sobor*"], i.e. the council of Muscovite high clergy, was an indispensable and organic part of the *zemskii sobor* together with state servitors [*sluzhilye liudi*] and those subject to governmental tax-ation and work [*tiaglye liudi*]. Going back still further into the past, to appanage [*udel'nyi*] times, we encounter "political" metropolitans who indicated to the petty Muscovite landowners the way of consolidating these lands and thus of building up Russia [*Rus'*]. Some were actual rulers of the Muscovite principality such as St. Aleksii.

However, all these well-known facts reveal only one side of Church-State relationships. In their one-sidedness these facts could even create the impression that the Church was simply used in governmental service — its honored enslavement. We want to be convinced that the Church preserved its independence and preserved in-corruptible its moral judgment in this difficult task of serving the government. In being so closely connected with the world, did the Church yet remain above the world as the preserver of different laws, as the mirror of another — the heavenly — truth?

Let us beware of two errors: excessive idealization of the past and painting it only black. In the past, as at

present, there was the eternal battle between good and
evil forces, between truth and falsehood, but, like now,
weakness and faint-heartedness prevailed over both good
and evil. We may observe that examples of the Church's
courageous lessons to the government, frequent in the
appanage era of Russian history, become less frequent in
the centuries of Muscovite autocracy. It was easy for the
Church to teach the love of peace and the loyalty of oath
to violent, though weak, princes who were not overly
bound to the land and were torn by internecine wars.
But the Grand Prince, and later Tsar of Muscovy, became
a "stern" and "formidable" sovereign who did not like
"confrontations" and did not tolerate defiance of his
will. And hence the Church's voice in the governmental
palace became quieter, more muted. Without accusation
or threat, the Church, in the person of the Metropolitan
and Patriarch, grieved for those in disfavor, trying to
soften the cruelty of governmental reason . . .

But there was that time when the Church courageously raised its voice directly before the face of the
"Terrible Tsar" and at one of the most tragic moments
in Russian history. During the years of bloody revolution
created by the sovereign, Metropolitan Filipp rose up
against the tyrant, ultimately paying with his life for
his fearless profession of truth and justice. St. Filipp
became a martyr not for the *faith* of Christ — the defender of which Ivan Vasil'evich [Ivan the Terrible] also
fancied himself to be — but for the *justice* and *truth*
of Christ which the Tsar had offended. He was practically
alone among contemporary hierarchs in his protest, almost
alone through the centuries as well. But his voice compensated for the silence of many. His feat is enough to
reveal a new trait in the image of Orthodoxy. The Church,
in canonizing this saint, took his feat — so rare even to the
present — upon itself. Metropolitan Filipp's feat also gives

true meaning to the service of his co-priests in Moscow's
Cathedral of the Assumption: St. Aleksii and St. Germogen. One saint gave the entirety of his life's labor to
the strengthening of the Muscovite state; the other gave
his life in defending it against internal enemies. St. Filipp
gave his life in a struggle with this very government in the
person of the Tsar. He showed that the government too
must be subordinated to the higher principles of life.
From St. Filipp's feat we understand that Russian saints
did not serve the mighty Muscovite secular power but
rather they served the light of Christ which shone in the
Tsardom — and only while this light shone.

In thus approaching the image and activity of St.
Filipp we are convinced that we are not being tendentious.
The hagiographical work on St. Filipp was structured in
this way: the role of the accuser of Ivan the Terrible overshadows the role of the monk from the Solovetskii monastery. For the consciousness of the ancient Russian
Church St. Filipp lives on in the memory as the Metropolitan of Moscow and not as the hermit from the White
Sea. Unfortunately there is only meager detail about his
inner spiritual traits. Nevertheless enough traits are given
which allow us to discern within his personal, monastic
path that aspect of his life which was devoted to the
service of society. Moreover St. Filipp belongs to those
figures whose personality is totally expressed in their
"exploit" or "feat." For this reason our biographical
experiment will be the experiment of the historian and
not the hagiographer. We shall attempt to compensate
for the paucity of personal traits in the biography by
placing it in an historical framework. Acquaintance with
the epoch may shed light on the meaning of the individual
feat. Metropolitan Filipp belongs as much to the history
of the Russian Church as to that of the Russian State.
It is not for naught that Karamzin saw in him a "hero,"

even "the most famous hero of ancient and modern history." We shall see that, as a true saint, he was also a humble hero who did not intentionally seek out the "feat." But, when the tortuous burden of the State fell upon his shoulders, St. Filipp did not avoid it. In fact, his previous labors had actually prepared him for accepting the burden.

CHAPTER ONE

IN THE MOSCOW
PALACE

St. Filipp was born on June 5, 1507. His worldly name was Fedor Stepanovich Kolychov. By birth he belonged to the ancient line of middle class Moscow boyars but not to the line of princely boyars. Their ancestors had long served the Moscow princes. The Zakhar'-ins (Romanovs), Sheremetevs and Kolychovs traced their lineage to the same ancestor. For years, together with the descendants of [Ivan] Kalita, they built up the state of Muscovy. Being a bit squeezed by the appanage princes, who began serving Muscovy from the time of Ivan III, they nevertheless continued their service to their sovereigns. Fedor's grandfather, Ivan Andreevich Kolychov-Lobanov, who went to the Crimea as an emissary of Ivan III, was vicegerent [*namestnik*] in Novgorod and served in the military. He was involved in campaigns against the Swedes and the Livonians and was killed in 1502 during a Livonian attack on Ivangorod. His son — and Fedor's father— the boyar Stepan Ivanovich, nicknamed *Stenstur*, was assigned as "uncle" (tutor) of Grand Prince Iurii Vasil'evich, the brother of Ivan the Terrible. Fedor's uncle, Ivan, headed the "council" of Prince Andrei Ivanovich Staritskii, an appanage prince of the Moscow house and the brother of Vasilii III. Serving him, he still served the family of the Moscow princes and only strife between the Moscow government and the appanage relatives placed him, as we shall see, in the ranks of Moscow's opposition.

This family-class reference does not seem superfluous in a biographical account of Metropolitan Filipp. More than once the fate of the Kolychovs became tragically intertwined with his own fate. The disfavor of the Kolychovs coincides with young Fedor's withdrawal from the world. The deposition of the metropolitan is accompanied by executions of Kolychovs. With the paucity of biographical information, others have thought it feasible to tie in Filipp's opposition to the Tsar with the opposition of the persecuted boyars. We shall see that there is a basic error in placing the question in such terms. But, although we refuse to consider the case of St. Filipp as a strictly political matter, we can repeat Ilovaiskii's observation that perhaps the fact of boyar origin was not accidental in the saint's biography.

We know almost nothing of the first thirty years of Fedor Kolychov's life. His mother, Varvara, ended her life in a monastery, taking her vows after her son. Her inherited estates were in the Novgorod district as were, of course, many of the Kolychovs'. Besides Fedor she also had three younger sons. Fedor learned to read and write at an early age. He also received the necessary military training expected of a boyar. He "rode horses from an early age." The *Life* of St. Filipp asserts that he was "not squeamish about it." The *Life* underscores the youth's estrangement from games and from the habits of children his age. It also stresses his love for reading, especially the reading of the lives of the "worthy fathers." The *Life* also notes that the youth "learned military courage also." A young boyar son could not but serve the sovereign. The *Life*, however, places his entry into service only with the commencement of Ivan III's reign. Actually this is one of the many inaccuracies of the *Life*. It is difficult to think that the youth did not serve

at all until the age of twenty-six. Perhaps the note in the
Life refers to Fedor's service in the Palace. Until that
time he could have been in the military and engaged in
campaigns. But no evidence regarding this has been preserved. It is also not known whether Fedor actually
arrived at the Palace only after the death of Grand Prince
Vasilii. His father and uncle were close to the Moscow
Court and it is unlikely that such a long wait would
have been necessary in order to place the young Kolychov
in one of the honorable and much promising courtly
duties. What service could Fedor have had at the Court?

After Ivan III's marriage to the Byzantine princess,
the Moscow Court broke with the patriarchal simplicity of
the appanage court in order to create an atmosphere of
magnificence which would impress foreign emissaries who
now began to appear in Moscow. The structure and scope
of courtly ranks increased. Under Ivan III — in addition
to the already existing courtly status of the boyars and
courtiers [*okol'nichie*] — the treasurer [*kaznachei*], the
chamberlain [*postel'nichii*], and the equerry [*koniushii*]
gained courtly status. Under Vasilii III we encounter in
addition the arms bearer [*oruzhnichii*], the hunting
master [*lovchii*], the banquet-chief [*kraichii*], aides
[*striapchie*], body guards [*ryndy*], assistant body guards
[*podryndy*], and lower officials. We must imagine Fedor
moving up the ladder of these courtly duties, conscious of
court customs and looking after the Grand Prince and
the people around him. If the youth was gifted with a
sensitive conscience, he had to evaluate and judge this
world. Let us attempt to reconstruct those impressions
which aided in the development of his character and
views. A thirteen year gap in his biography gives us enough
time and place to fill it in with a cursory look at political
and ecclesiastical relations as they were formed in Moscow
at the beginning of the 16th century. We present these

facts in the light in which they were actually seen by the more sensitive — morally and politically — contemporaries from the boyar and ecclesiastical circles.

The rule of Vasilii III does not belong to the most brilliant or most tragically tense pages of Russian history. But in all respects it fittingly takes its place between the rules of both "terrible" Ivans — the grandfather and the grandson. It emerges from the pages of the chronicles as a time of tense struggle and work, growing power, and preparation for future accomplishments. The Russian Tsardom ripens with its inherent potential for empire. The great Moscow principality is reborn as Russia. It is in the reign of Vasilii III that a Pskovian monk, Filofei, one of the first Muscovite publicists, expresses his views on Moscow as the successor of Byzantium and the bearer of the Orthodox kingdom—the Third Rome. "Two Romes have fallen, a third stands, and a fourth there will not be."

In reading the historians of this time, one is amazed at the quantity of effort spent, of blood spilled on all the borders of the Russian land. Border war is practically without interruption: with Kazan', the Crimea, Lithuania. Serious setbacks (near Kazan' and by the Orsha) are inter-mixed with splendid successes — Smolensk is forever re-turned into the structure of the Russian state. Observing the price paid for successes, one understands that the building of the Muscovite Tsardom must take on a stern style: the enserfment of service and obligation.

In the path of the new national goal stand the last principalities — more correctly, the shadow of former principalities and independent cities — Riazan', Pskov and others. They retained the old law [staroe pravo] which, consequently, meant for ancient Russian man the re-tention of the "moral law" [nravstvennaia pravda]. In the name of national interest, Moscow was not embar-rassed to trample upon the law [pravda]. That a national consciousness, an over-all Russian concern, was not foreign to the princely house of Moscow may be seen by the words — according to Tatishchev — of Grand Prince Ivan III to the metropolitan, who had previously asked for the release of Ivan's brother, Prince Andrei:

> I am sorry for my brother but I cannot free him . . . When I die, he will seek to attain grand princely rule under my nephew, and if he does not achieve it himself, he will create discord among my children, and they will fight with each other. The Tatars will begin to destroy the Russian land, burn and enslave, and again impose tribute. Christian blood will flow as before and all my efforts will be in vain. You will be slaves of the Tatars.

Thus, for the sake of national effort, the most difficult sacrifices were made, not only of labor and blood but of conscience. It seems as if the lessons of Italian diplomats of the Machiavellian school were adopted in Moscow together with the appearance of the Duchess of Ferrara, educated in Rome (Sophia), and together with Western diplomatic embassies.

These political lessons of the Western Renaissance are echoed by the obsequious voices of the "Josephite" Church party (students of Iosif of Volotsk) which justified the "wise perfidy" ["*bogopremudrostnoe kovarstvo*"] of the sovereign.

The fate of the principalities best shows how these lessons of "wise perfidy" were applied in practice. The last grand prince of Riazan', Ivan, was put in a dungeon in Moscow from which he fled to Lithuania during the invasion of Moscow by Mehmet-Girei, the Crimean Khan. Prince Vasilii Ivanovich Shemiachich, nephew of Shemiaka and Prince of Novgorod-Severskii, ended his life in a

Moscow dungeon. Pskov lost its independence in 1510 not
because of a revolt or a political clash with Moscow. It was
caught treacherously, by surprise, in the style of Caesar
Borgia. It is instructive to compare the legal and moral
basis of Ivan III's campaign against Novgorod with the
overthrow of Pskov by his son. For a long time Ivan de-
layed and endured Novgorodian offenses. Novgorod's
national treachery (union with Lithuania) gave him an
excellent excuse to make a move in 1471. Russia's national
consciousness was with the Moscow Prince. Vasilii III
promised the people of Pskov to hear personally their
complaints against his vicegerent [namestnik]. He summoned the boyars and the "worthiest people" [luchshie
liudi] of Pskov to Novgorod as plaintiffs and unexpectedly
ordered their arrest. The Moscow boyars cynically stated
to the people of Pskov. "You have been caught by God
and by Grand Prince Vasilii Ivanovich of all Russia."
Deprived of its leaders, Pskov did not resist. With bent
knee it met its "conqueror" — ("Pskov was taken without
struggle"). The city pulled down its bell of the popular
assembly [vechevoi kolokol] and accompanied its exiles
to Moscow. Then the defenseless and loyal Russian city
was deliberately given to Moscow military commanders
[voevody] and bureaucrats [d'iaki] for plunder.

In the Shemiachich affair the perfidy of Moscow's
politics also compromises the dignity of the Church.
Prince Shemiachich, whose territory bordered Lithuania,
although loyal to Moscow, aroused Moscow's suspicion.
Prince Starodubskii, the neighbor and age-old rival of
Shemiachich, fed these suspicions at the court of the
Grand Prince. Having been summoned to Moscow for
explanation, Shemiachich was able to defend himself
against the accusations. But, when he was summoned a
second time, he was troubled and asked for guarantees
of "safe passage" ["opasnaia gramota"]. These "safe

passages" promised him an unimpeded return and were
given by Vasilii and Metropolitan Daniil. Despite this,
Shemiachich was arrested in Moscow and incarcerated in
one of the Kremlin towers where he died. It is told that
during his stay in Moscow a holy fool [*iurodivyi*] walked
the streets with a broom, saying: "the Sovereign's land is
not yet wholly cleansed — now is the time to clean up the
remaining litter." Evidently public consciousness supported the Moscow prince in the matter of cleaning up
the appanage "litter." But those who stood behind the
scenes of Muscovite politics and still believed in the
sacredness of an oath could not but be outraged, especially
by the participation of Metropolitan Daniil in this matter.
The hierarch was taken into the conspiracy against the
Severskii prince and consciously supported it. Later he
even had the boldness to justify his action. In a conversation with the boyar Bersen he said: "God rid him (the
Grand Prince) of an enemy within." "Who is this enemy?"
"Shemiachich." "He forgot," adds Bersen, "how he had
written the letter [of safe passage] with his signature and
seal, and had sworn on the icon of the Virgin and the
Miracle-Worker, and upon his soul."

It was not only the appanage princes who died as
sacrifices to Moscow's politics. Dimitrii, the nephew of
Ivan III, met the same fate as Prince Shemiachich and the
Prince of Riazan'. He was the legal heir to the throne,
the first to be coronated in Moscow according to the
triumphal Byzantine custom by which, later, Ivan the
Terrible was coronated. The struggle of courtly factions,
the victory of the famous Sophia Paleologos — the sovereign's second wife — led the eight year old Prince Dimitrii to a Kremlin dungeon. He simply had to give up
his place to his fortunate rival, Vasilii, the son of the
Greek woman. The young prisoner, like Emperor Ivan
Antonovich, languished for a long time in the Kremlin

tower, and although the report of his forced death is
evidently unjust, he died "in need" — in the words of
the chronicler — in 1509, casting a dark shadow on the
glitter of the Muscovite Court. Vasilii III could not perform the crowning ceremony on himself. He could not do
it without bringing to the people's conscience and memory
the one to whom Church ritual had already given the
stamp of "imperial" consecration.

Triumphing over his enemies and destroying the
appanage system, the Prince of Moscow broke those
patriarchal traditions of his power and of his closest
associates which now seemed to be incompatible with
autocracy. Former simplicity was replaced by magnificent
ceremony. The old boyars who built the Muscovite State
and who stood totally behind their prince did not hesitate
to oppose his will. They considered their participation in
the princely council to be their right and the basis of
the structure of government. Now they were condemned
to yield their place to court favorites. Vasilii was arrogant
and unsociable with them. He was capable of chasing a
sharply critical adviser from his council: "Get out, you
peasant; I don't need you." "Our sovereign is stubborn,"
complains one of the fallen advisors, "and does not like
to be contradicted. Whoever contradicts him finds himself
in disfavor. But his father liked to be contradicted and
favored those who did so." "Our sovereign has locked
himself in for three days now and takes care of all matters
by himself from his bed." In these deviations from the
past, people were prepared to see a dangerous break in
government. "The land which changes its customs does
not last long. Our Grand Prince has changed our old
customs, and what good will this bring for us?" Thus
speaks Bersen. And *d'iak* Zharenyi echoes this, referring
now to the personal character of the Grand Prince: "Our
sovereign is cruel and unkind." Maxim the Greek, a foreign

witness for whom Russia became a step-mother and a second homeland, also noted the last characteristic:"As the sovereign goes to church, the widows cry and follow him, and they (the sovereign's retinue) beat them." Such talk took place surreptitiously in Moscow chambers and we do not know, of course, how indicative it was of public opinion. But, paying heed to the fact that it could cost the careless his tongue (Zharenyi), or even his head (Bersen), need we be amazed that news of it comes to us so obscurely?

Herberstein, the Imperial (German) ambassador who came to Moscow twice in Vasilii III's reign, says that in his power the Muscovite sovereign exceeds all other monarchs in the world. "He uses his power in relation to clerics just as he uses it with laymen. Freely, and according to his will, he commands the life and property of all. Not one of his advisers has an authority such that he dare to disagree with him or contradict him in a particular matter." Herberstein is amazed by the theocratic character of this power. It is expressed in enunciations and proverbs he heard which seemingly do not distinguish the person of the sovereign from God. "The sovereign's will is God's will"; "God and the great sovereign know of this." According to Herberstein, the Russians even call the Grand Prince "God's chamberlain and house-keeper." The foreigner correctly observed the juridically limitless power of the prince (not even the Tsar). Its connection to moral and religious law could not but fail to escape him, especially in the atmosphere of courtly flattery. Violation of it, particularly in the presence of the theocratic ideal of power, had to be painfully perceived. Nevertheless, in Herberstein's *Description of Muscovy* there is the reflection of the sharp break in social relations experienced in the reigns of Ivan III and Vasilii III.

It remains to discuss the Church side of this break which could not but affect the future monk and saint. Actually, hardly anyone in the Moscow of the sixteenth century could remain alien to Church interests and the burning questions of the day. In essence, all internal events, the whole struggle of factions and ideas which filled Vasilii's reign — these were expressed in the struggle on Church matters. The heresy of the Judaizers was living out its day, not yet finished off by the executions and oppression under Ivan III. This strange movement was the echo of Western Reformation ferment in its various forms — pure Judaism and religious rationalism and free thought. Primarily it infected the upper crust of Muscovite society and of the Church. It had its adherents at Court, in the family of the Grand Prince (Elena, the bride of Ivan III), and even in the metropolitan's seat in the person of Zosima who was deposed as metropolitan in 1494 "due to his own infirmity." Concerning the treatment of the heresy — more accurately, the measures to combat it — the Church was divided. Iosif, the hegumen of Volokolamsk, the stern zealot, demanded executions. But Ivan's conscience balked at the shedding of blood in matters of faith. Iosif insisted strongly at the Council of 1504 and achieved the condemnation of the heretics. Many of them were then burned in Moscow and Novgorod. Princess Elena died in a dungeon. Unhappy with just the executions of the obstinate, Iosif also fought against the acceptance of the repentant back into the Church. He did not believe in the sincerity of their repentance. In considering them to be not mere heretics but apostates from Christianity, he reminded people of the laws of the ancient Church according to which apostates were condemned to lifetime repentance. In addition to many epistles, Iosif compiled an extensive work against the heretics entitled *"The Enlightener"* [*"Prosvetitel'"*]. When the Judaizers, having recovered from the repressions, again began to raise their heads, Iosif wrote a tearful message to Vasilii III (1511-1512). "For the sake of God and the Virgin, care for and think of the holy churches and the Orthodox faith, and of us, your poor and your destitute ones . . . As before, you, God's anointed sovereign are like the pious Prince Constantine and, together with your father, you put down the evil Novgorod heretics and apostates. And now if you, sovereign, will not take the trouble and move to crush their dark, heretical teaching, then as a result all Orthodox Christianity will be destroyed. When your father damned the heretics Zakharii and Dionisii, he had them locked in a dungeon. There they died and attracted no Orthodox. But those who began to repent, those whom your father believed, created much evil and enticed many Christians into Judaism. Only you, sovereign and autocrat of all the Russian land, can end this misfortune." The Grand Prince displayed zeal and "ordered all heretics to be thrown in the dungeon and kept there to the end of their days. Hearing of this, the hegumen father praised God — Father, Son, and Holy Spirit."

From Iosif's above-cited letter we observe the lofty value he placed on grand princely power. "The divine prince and autocrat," according to the idea of the letter, is the heir of Constantine's kingdom and cause. Loyalty to the autocratic idea constitutes the distinguishing trait of all Iosif's students and followers — the whole Josephite party which became predominant in the reign of Vasilii III. Religious conservatism and a loyalty to the reigning powers unite with social and domestic conservatism. The Josephites were fiery defenders of Church estates and of the right of monasteries to rule over settled lands. These Church estates were being pressured from all sides at the beginning of the sixteenth century — there was pressure from the ascetically motivated representatives of monasticism, from the ruling boyar circles, and from the State which was thinking of secularizing monastic lands.

The question of monastic properties was raised at the Council of 1503 by the "Trans-Volga Elders." This was the name given to the hermits who lived in Belozersk and other northern hermitages. Nil Sorskii, the leader of this party, began to say that "monasteries should not maintain villages, that the monks should live in the wilderness and that they should feed themselves by their own labor." His view on this was sternly ascetical. The Trans-Volga elders were "non-possessors" ["*nestia-zhateli*"], opponents of the economic growth of monasteries in which they perceived the source of secularization and social injustice (oppression of peasants). In their lofty spirituality the Trans-Volga elders far exceeded the Josephites. In his devotional works St. Nil Sorskii has left us — and he is almost the only one in ancient Russia to do so — a school of spiritual work, of "mental prayer," — that is, of purely spiritual contemplation.

These Trans-Volga elders came out against the execution of heretics, upholding — if not freedom of conscience — then a magnanimous attitude toward the repentant. Agreeing that "stubborn and unrepenting heretics be incarcerated," they contended that "repentant heretics who condemned their own heresy would be accepted by God's Church with open arms." They even asserted that the heretics should not be sought out if they kept to their heresy in secret and did not spread it among the Orthodox. Their lenient attitude toward the heretics reached the point where the elders gave them sanctuary in their hermitages and opponents accused some of them of open sympathy for the heresy.

Boyar circles hated the Josephites and Prince Kurb-skii calls them nothing other than "despicable and cunning." The boyars supported the position of the Trans-

Volga elders in the question of Church properties and in
the handling of heretics. Of course their sympathy for the
"non-possessors" flowed from their selfish motive of
jealousy of privileged patrimonies. They sympathized with
the repressed heretics primarily because they were in sympathy with freedom of thought. Actually, these two
opposing tendencies — the boyar and the ascetical — sometimes intertwined fancifully in the published works of that
time. In the prince-monk Vassian Kosom (Patrikeev), a
well-known boyar who was forcibly tonsured under Ivan
III, it is difficult to distinguish what comes from the spirit
of "non-possession" and what derives from the boyar
dislike of rich monks. If the boyar party used the "non-
possessors," then the supporters of autocracy also used
the Josephites. Political and social conflicts were inex-
tricably tied up with religious problems. It is this which
gave the age — in the entirety of its spiritual life — an
amazing tenseness and the possibility of moving in various
directions, a characteristic of all great turning points in
history.

Toward the end of Vasilii's rule, the Josephites won
out. The expression of this victory was the synodical condemnation and exile of Vassian and of his personal friend
Maxim the Greek (1531). It was not only the party of
Church defenders which triumphed. Also triumphant was
the new idea (in Russia) of autocracy.

This autocracy, much in the style of all old Russian
life, wished to rest upon indigenous, ancient law. On his
death bed Vasilii III could tell his boyars: "You yourselves
know that our government over Vladimir, Novgorod and
Moscow traces itself back to Grand Prince Vladimir of
Kiev. We are your born rulers and you are our age-long
boyars." This, however, did not impede this same Vasilii
from causing a fundamental break not only in the relationship of the sovereign to the boyars but also of the sov-

ereign to the Church.

That same observant foreigner whose *Description of
Muscovy* we have already cited, witnesses: "Formerly,
metropolitans and archbishops were elected by a synod of
all archbishops, bishops, archimandrites and hegumens.
The more holy ones were sought out in monasteries and
hermitages and they were elected. But the present sovereign, they say, usually attracts to himself those persons
he knows well and then he selects one of them on the basis
of his own judgment." Herberstein's observation is corrob-
orated by historians of the Russian Church. Under Vasilii
two metropolitans were chosen. Varlaam (1511) and
Daniil (1521). The chronicles do not mention Varlaam's
election. They state only that on July 27 he was taken to
the metropolitan's court and appointed metropolitan, and
on August 3 he was assigned to a metropolitanate. Only at
this last ceremonial act were bishops present. But, no
matter how Varlaam was chosen, there is no doubt that he
was removed forcibly from the post. The chronicle states
that he "left the metropolitanate and went to Simonov
(i.e. Simonov Monastery), and from Simonov he was exiled
to the Vologodskii district, to Kameni" (the Kamenyi
Monastery at Lake Kubenskoe). Herberstein writes that
the reason for the metropolitan's removal was the Prince's
'oath-breaking' in the famed Shemiachich affair, together
with "other matters which seemed to be contrary to the
metropolitan's dignity and rule." He personally gave his
bishop's crozier to the Prince. The Prince, having allegedly
put him in chains, sent him to a monastery. Since Shemiachich was taken two years after Varlaam's removal,
Herberstein's story cannot be accurate. If the Shemiachich
affair was one of the reasons for the metropolitan's disfavor, then it means that he did not wish to do what was
demanded of him; that is, to take the sin upon his conscience, something which his complaisant successor under-

took.

In the person of Daniil, a Josephite, the Grand Prince obtained a hierarch of his taste. a brilliant orator, a writer, and one who was strict with heretics but yet condescending to the sovereign's weaknesses. Herberstein passes on the most unflattering rumors which went about Moscow. The metropolitan was still young, was burly but handsome with a rosy face. "In order not to appear more concerned with eating than fasting, vigil, and prayer, he fumigated his face with sulphuric smoke so that he would look paler." This is, however, rumor and gossip. Still, it is noteworthy that St. Iosif of Volotsk, in selecting a successor for the cloister, gave the Grand Prince ten names. Daniil was not among them. Nevertheless, Daniil was chosen to be hegumen of Iosif's monastery from which the Prince elevated him to the Moscow Metropolitanate.

Bersen, whom we have already met, complains to Maxim the Greek. "I do not understand whether he is a metropolitan or just a plain monk. One does not hear a learned word from him and he does not concern himself with anyone. Former bishops [sviatiteli], while occupying their Sees, interceded [pechalovalis'] on behalf of all people to the sovereign." Bersen is not quite fair. Metropolitan Daniil was more "learned" than many of his predecessors which is proven by many of his sermons and accusations. But it is difficult to imagine this obliging hierarch in the role of a sincere "intercessor" ["pechalovatel'"]. The spiritual independence of the Church and the loftiness of its moral truth were expressed most strongly in the Church's ancient custom of intercession [Pechalovanie] on behalf of the disfavored and the accused. Supporting the Moscow sovereigns in their gathering of Russian lands and not denying their sovereigns the right to punish the disobedient autocratically, the supreme hierarchs took upon themselves the noble role of advocates of mercy. The cruelty of political necessity and of party strife was mitigated by the Church's mercy. In the sixteenth century, with the sharply heightened consciousness of the new sovereigns, intercession [*pechalovanie*] — and we shall see this in the reign of Ivan the Terrible —becomes a difficult feat for the representatives of the Church. It is quite feasible that Daniil had no wish to burden himself with "intercession." We have observed the case in which he took upon himself the sin of perjury in the Shemiachich affair. Contemporaries also blamed him for complicity in another sin, and a sin which was by no means insignificant for the religious conscience of Muscovites —.the sovereign's divorce of his wife Solomonia. The sole reason for the divorce was the childlessness of the Grand Princess, a reason not accepted by the Church. The Prince justified the divorce on grounds of political necessity, mistrust of his brothers who were to inherit the government after him: "They cannot even rule over their own principalities." It is strange that historians too accept the weightiness of this naive notion. The traits of an unborn heir cannot be determined. In leaving the government to his infant son rather than to his brother, Vasilii III inevitably entrusted the government into weak, female hands which were held by powerful, though selfish boyars, both relatives and favorites.

The boyars' time of troubles [*smutnoe vremia*] during Ivan IV's infancy and the destructive influence of this on Ivan the Terrible's character — all this was the consequence of Vasilii III's "political" divorce. The Church was asked to bless this doubtful political and moral action. Wishing to obtain blessing for his uncanonical act, the Grand Prince — it is said — sent letters to all the Eastern Patriarchs and to Mt. Athos. Supposedly the Greeks replied with a decisive refusal. The Metropolitan of Moscow took this sin also upon himself as his responsibil-

ity. Solomonia was not only divorced from her husband
with whom she had lived in peace and harmony for twenty
years but also forcibly tonsured as a nun. It is said that
during the act of tonsuring [*postrizhenie*] there were cruel
scenes in the Church. The Princess trampled the cowl
[*kukol'*] which the metropolitan gave to her, screamed
that she was being forcibly tonsured, and called upon God
the avenger. Ivan Shigona, the Grand Prince's representa-
tive at this sad ritual, supposedly dared to raise his hand
against the unfortunate one — according to Herberstein.

In any case, whether or not these details are true,
this affair had to produce a deep impression on the Muscovites who were devoted to the faith, canons, and regulations of the Church. The blasphemous divorces of Ivan
the Terrible were prepared by this first transgression of
his father.

In all these events we see the expression of one
common historical phenomenon: the diminishing of the
independence of spiritual rule simultaneous with the
growth of the Moscow autocratic consciousness of the
Moscow sovereigns. It is not so much a question of the
personal character traits of Vasilii III and Metropolitan
Daniil. This tendency is apparent when one observes the
events of the five reigns from the middle of the fifteenth
century to the end of the sixteenth century. It is particularly vividly expressed in the fate of the metropolitanate's
power. Let us turn our attention to only one striking fact.
The forcible deposition of Varlaam from the metropolitan's seat was a totally new phenomenon in the history of
the Russian Church. Up to the middle of the fifteenth
century, all Russian metropolitans were either Greeks sent
from Constantinople or they were appointed by the ecu-
menical patriarchs from the candidates proposed by the
Muscovite and Western Russian princes. The Grand Prince
of Moscow, although not possessing the right to independ-

ently appoint a metropolitan, could nevertheless depose him. This act of deposition demanded, however, a formal patriarchal trial in Constantinople. This independence from local rule raised the primate of the Russian Church above all the political powers in Russia. In relationship to the princes, he was a fatherly figure, though not always impartial or inimical to a specific political policy — that is, protection of Moscow's growing autocracy. Having attained their goals with the help of the Church, the Moscow princes began to chafe under its patriarchal tutelage. We can already see friction under the first autocrat-sovereign, Ivan III. For many years the Grand Prince quarreled with Metropolitan Gerontii on a purely ecclesiastical question (religious processions [*khozhdenie "posolon' "*]). As a result the Grand Prince caused Gerontii's departure from the metropolitanate. When the metropolitan, exhausted by the struggle and worn out by illness, left for a monastery without renouncing his position of metropolitan, the Grand Prince began attempting to obtain his formal abdication. Gerontii, however, did not succumb to the entreaties and returned to the metropolitanate. The sovereign had to give in on everything, including the liturgical question which had separated them. We do not speak here of Zosima's abdication. He was clearly a heretic and in his case great care was taken. Instead of a conciliar denunciation to which his confederates were subjected, he was given the opportunity of stepping down "because of infirmity."

Vasilii III could dare something which had held back his "terrible" father. Metropolitan Varlaam became the first victim of the new relationship. When the precedent was established, it began to be used with extraordinary ease. Daniil, knowing how to please Vasilii III, was removed from the position of metropolitan during the boyar years just like his predecessor Iosif. The proud and learned bishop even had to sign an unheard of humiliating document [*gramota*] at his abdication.

If we observe the nine hierarchs who occupied the Moscow metropolitanate during the time of Vasilii III and Ivan IV, we shall see that only three of them died in office. The others were forcibly deprived of it or "voluntarily" abdicated. One of them (St. Filipp) also lost his life as well as the metropolitanate. Abdications continue under the humble Fedor Ivanovich, indicating a firmly established tradition.

These were the political, ecclesiastical and social turning points which took place in the Moscow of Vasilii III and formed the background for the youth of Fedor Kolychov. Almost all these events took place before his eyes. He probably knew personally most of the personages of this age, an age rich in disturbance. Close to the grand princely Court, he had to take to heart all that troubled his contemporaries. These considerations justify our lengthy introduction to his biography. We proceed from the assumption that political and ecclesiastical events cultivated his character and his convictions. In what spirit and in what direction? This, of course, we cannot determine with certainty. But with a great deal of probability, it can be assumed that because of his lineage and membership in the boyar circle as well as his later clerical affiliation it is unlikely that he could be in the camp of the new regime's admirers. Not belonging to the close circles of the Grand Prince's favorites, he was probably more accessible to the muted murmers against it which also reached foreign ears. Later, in accusing the son, Metropolitan Filipp set the father as an example. Time—and the cruelties of Ivan IV—could erase from memory, and even rehabilitate, the sternness of his father's reign. In the same way the contemporaries of Vasilii thought of Ivan III's time as ideal—a time of patriarchal character, of simplicity, and of truth. The boyar contemporaries of Ivan III, however, judged this quite differently.

The historian of the State, enchanted by the growth of external power and the might of Moscow, will view this picture as tendentious, as the darker side of a great historical process. In Metropolitan Filipp's biography this picture is doubly justified: as the perception of the environment to which the young Kolychov belonged and as the background in which the figure of the future metropolitan can boldly appear.

After the death of Vasilii, matters in Moscow were particularly stormy and troublesome. Many of the Kolychovs were caught up in this whirlpool. Since the catastrophe which overtook this boyar family is directly connected with the most important turning point in Fedor's destiny, we have to look in more detail at the five year regency of Elena (1533-1538).

With the regency of Elena Glinskaia imperious foreign influence on Russian government life occurs again. When dying, the Grand Prince willed to her the State and the infant son. Elena was the niece of the famous Lithuanian magnate, Prince Michael, a leading adventurer who left his traces — those of a condottiere — on the political history of Western Europe. Prince Glinskii served many European monarchs — in Italy, in Spain, and at the court of Emperor Maximilian. In Lithuania, under Grand Prince Alexander, the "little court marshal" ruled over almost half the government. Evidently his goal was to become the independent ruler of the Western Russian lands. Having been crushed in these notions under King Sigismund, he went over to the service of the Moscow prince, hoping to be given the principality of Smolensk. When these hopes likewise did not materialize, he attempted to cross back into Lithuania but was caught and placed in a Kremlin dungeon. Vasilii III's marriage to Glinskii's niece freed

Glinskii and placed him at the head of Moscow's aristocracy. During the first years of Elena's regency, he was the
chief figure in the strata of boyar rule.

With Princess Elena and her family, a fresh spirit of
the Renaissance breaks into Moscow. This time the spirit
is not Italo-Greek but Polish-Western. Princess Elena must
have received an excellent education. Perhaps this is why
the Grand Prince preferred her to the women from the
families of Moscow boyars. Unfortunately, we know
nothing of the positive cultural influence which came from
the Glinskii family. We hear only that the Grand Prince, to
please his young wife, shaved off his beard — a Western
fashion which had spread among the Moscow dandies and
which caused indignation among the adherents of the
"old way." In addition to beard shaving, Elena—it seems—
brought with her a general atmosphere of immorality to
the princely chamber in the Kremlin. At least her short
rule is rich in scandal and dark deeds. Moscow resented
her almost open liason with Prince Telepnev-Ovchina
(Obolenskii) who played the role of a favorite at Court.
Prince Michael himself, uncle of the ruler, fell in a struggle
with this Court favorite. Elena sent him (1534) to the
same tower from which she had earlier liberated him, to
the tower "past the Neglin and Iamskii court." Soon
after he died there.

The departure to Lithuania of the Prince of Bel'sk
and Liatsk led to the arrest of boyars suspected of complicity. Most tragic of all was the fate of Iurii and Andrei,
appanage princes and brothers of the deceased sovereign.
Vasilii III died on December 3, 1533. Eight days after his
death, Prince Iurii Dmitrovskii, who had come to Moscow
during the sovereign's fateful illness, was seized. He was
accused of enticing Prince Andrei Shuiskii into his service.
This, however, concealed another accusation — the striving
for the Moscow throne. One of the chronicles expresses

this thought, attributing it to the boyars who surrounded the ruler: "If Prince Iurii Ivanovich was not seized, the government of the Grand Prince could not be strong. The sovereign is young, but Iurii is of age and can rule over people. If people come to him, he will seek to govern by the Grand Prince" (i.e. attempt to obtain the title of Grand Prince). This chronicler is clearly not sympathetic to the Moscow government: "The devil placed this evil thought in the boyars knowing that if Prince Iurii was not seized, then his (the devil's) will would not come about in plunder, betrayal and murder." Plunder and killings are pictured as inevitable consequences of the sovereign's infancy and the rule of favorites. In any case, the public consciousness was divided in this conflict just as it was divided, if we judge by the chronicles, at the fall of Prince Andrei. Prince Iurii, arrested because of the 'word' of the boyars, was put in the same tower where the unfortunate Dimitrii, Ivan's son, ended his life. He died in the dungeon after three years — from hunger, according to the words of the chronicle: "a death of suffering, in open need." (1536).

The fate of Andrei Staritskii was decided a few months after Prince Iurii's death. The youngest of Vasilii's brothers, his relationship with him was better than that of others. Being without political ambition, he was living out his life in Starits surrounded by his appanage court and boyars among whom, as we know, one of the top places was occupied by Ivan Kolychov, the uncle of the future metropolitan. After the forty day mourning period for his dead brother, he began to ask the ruler to allot him towns for his appanage. He was refused — however, in accordance with the custom of respect for the deceased, he was given fur coats and horses. The disaffection between the large Moscow Court and the small Starits Court began here. The whisperers and the turncoats awakened mutual suspicion.

Called to Moscow, Prince Andrei made peace with Elena. He swore "upon his own damnation" not to accept those who had been unloyal to the Grand Prince. But, after this, the disaffection, which had been temporarily suppressed, continued.

Brother Iurii's death obviously helped to hasten the outcome. On the occasion of the Kazan' campaign, Elena ordered the Prince of Starits to be summoned to Moscow. Citing illness, Andrei did not go. The foreign doctor, Feofil, was sent to him and reported that Andrei's illness was not severe. Elena demanded that he immediately come to Moscow no matter what his condition. The reply of the appanage prince has come down to us. Calling himself a "slave" ["*kholop*"] of the Grand Prince and humbly begging for mercy, he complained bitterly of injury: "in the past, sovereign, we were never carried to you sovereigns on stretchers."

In the meantime rumors reached Moscow that the Prince of Starits was planning flight. An embassy of three clerics from Metropolitan Daniil was sent to him. They tried to persuade him to "go to the sovereign without any doubt; and we will bless you and will welcome you into our hands." Daniil's proffered guarantee obviously inspired little confidence especially since regiments under the command of the two Obolenskii princes, Nikita the Lame and Ovchina, Elena's favorite, were already moving from Moscow toward Volok. On the second of May Andrei fled Starits and hurriedly began to gather those who were loyal to him. In letters to the landowners of Novgorod and to the lesser gentry, he wrote: "The Grand Prince is young, the government is in the hands of the boyars, so whom are you to serve? I will be glad to favor you." Many answered his call. But Prince Nikita had already gone to fortify Novgorod. Ovchina, who took up a position by the Volga, first blocked the road to Lithuania and then moved on to the chase and, having caught up with Prince Andrei's forces, persuaded them to surrender and place themselves at the mercy of Moscow. In the name of the ruler, Ovchina swore that the prince would not be seized in Moscow and that he would not fall into great disfavor. The Prince of Starits fell into a trap. In Moscow he was free for only two days. Then the ruler announced that the military commander was not authorized to give a guarantee to the prince and ordered him to be put in chains. The prince lived no more than half a year in captivity. The old tradition of Moscow's perfidy was, under Elena, continued with a system of secret executions. Under Elena, no one came out alive from the Kremlin towers.

The fall of the appanage prince led to executions and disgrace for his followers. His wife and his son, Vladimir, were put under guard. Appanage boyars — Princes Pronskii, Obolenskii, the Peninskiis, the Paletskiis, and with them the lesser gentry sitting in "the house and council" of Prince Andrei — were subjected to torture, wholesale execution, and incarceration. Finally, thirty landowners from Novgorod who went over to Prince Andrei were hanged and their gallows were placed along the whole road from Moscow to Novgorod. The chronicle cites many Kolychovs among them.

The unsuccessful revolt of Prince Staritskii, along with the executions which followed, occurred in May (1537). On the seventh of July, according to the words of St. Filipp's *Life*, the young Fedor was struck in Church by the words of the Gospel which claimed one could not serve two masters. Fedor then decided to leave the world. It would be difficult to deny any connection between these two events. But, in asserting it, we do not wish nor have the right to represent Fedor Kolychov as a conspirator against the Moscow government who fled to a monastery in order to save his own neck. We do not know whether any personal danger threatened him. Not all the Kolychovs suffered. Fedor's father, Stepan Ivanovich, as tutor to the sovereign's younger son, Iurii, was probably close to the sovereign. But the tragic death of relatives and dear ones was simply too much to bear. It was indeed difficult at that time to serve two masters in Moscow. Fedor saw enough of political life in Moscow to feel revulsion for it. There is one circumstance which forces the assumption of an earlier religious calling in the young Fedor. At the age of thirty Fedor was still unmarried, a surprising circumstance in Russia. The thought of renouncing the world might have been growing secretly within him for a long time. The political catastrophe only hastened his decision.

Quite frequently religious "conversion" occurs not without the influence of external, worldly motives. The means and ordeals by which God leads the soul along the path of purification from passions are diverse. Wordly losses — that is God's challenge to the soul; in such a situation will the soul of man collapse or will it be reborn? The life of the monk and metropolitan which follows answers the question of the true motive of his departure from the world; it reveals what was external and what was internal.

We feel still that the external, i.e. the painful political experience through which he lived in his youth was not merely negative. Revulsion for the world was not the only effect political events had on Fedor. Living through such political events, Fedor also gained a clear, sober evaluation of the complex powers by which the fabric of political events is woven. He had been placed in a position from which he could more clearly see behind the scenes of the historical theater. He saw the shadier sides of its actors, their intriques and passions which blend with their ideas of the public good and national glory. The historical break in Russian life ran like a cruel seam through his environment and through his family circle. It crushed his own career. He did not emerge from the crisis an embittered factionalist but a mature man who could see clearly both sides of the boundary, one who knew the value of things and how to distinguish the holy from the human. There could not be a better school for the future metropolitan. Yet its lessons had still to be supplemented by the lessons of spiritual life, that school on whose door he was knocking — this fugitive and pilgrim who left behind him the dangerous glitter of the Moscow Court.

CHAPTER TWO

SOLOVKI

We know of many disgraced boyars of the sixteenth century who exchanged the Tsar's Court for the monastery. We know how easy it was for a rich and influential man in any cloister to surround himself with the comfort and luxury with which a person in his position was accustomed. He could have many servants, his own barns, and his own cellars. With indignation, Ivan the Terrible tells of such noble and sweet life of the boyars in the Kirillov Monastery: "Sheremet'ev now sits in a cell as though a Tsar and Khabarov, together with other monks, comes and they eat and drink just as they did in the world. And Sheremet'ev sends pastilas, honey cakes, and various spiced vegetables to the cells as if this were a wedding or a christening. Beyond the monastery, Sheremet'ev has a household where he keeps all kinds of yearly provisions. . ." About the monk-prince Vassian who chose the Simonov Monastery in Moscow, his evil-wisher writes: "He drinks an incalculable quantity of romania, bastr, muscatel, and white Rhine wine."

It was not for this type of life that Kolychov left Moscow and the first steps of his ascetical path will reveal quite well the difference between those of noble background who became monks essentially against their will and those who become monks because it is their vocation, their calling. According to the *Life*, Fedor left Moscow without telling anyone of his departure, not even his parents. He took nothing for his journey except clothing, "necessary coverings." It is noteworthy that Fedor did not chose any of the known Trans-Volga monasteries. Nor did he choose a monastery near Moscow. Instead, he went to the distant Solovetskii Monastery on the White Sea. The way to Solovki is long and difficult. Fedor did not take the direct road which leads from Moscow through Vologda and along the Dvina. He took a roundabout route which went through the surroundings of Novgorod. The reasons for the digression are not known — perhaps it was because of close family ties in Novgorod, or perhaps he had not actually decided at that time to journey to the northern monastery at Solovki. But we do find him later at Lake Onega which is the halfway point between Novgorod and the White Sea. The roads were along lakes and swamps and hence these roads were inaccessible in summer. One had to go by boat or else await winter when the frost would freeze the unstable quagmires. Some unknown reason — perhaps the absence of passageway, perhaps the lack of means — forced Fedor to stop at the shore of Lake Onega at the village of Kizh (or Khizh). Here he stayed for "quite a few" days at the home of a local settler, Subbota, and was — for this short time — a herdsman. Thus, the future shepherd of "talking sheep" first had to watch over "wordless sheep," as the *Life* notes. The boyar son immediately experienced the cup of need and deprivation. To work as a village shepherd was — for the former courtier — a better 'school of humility' than any monastic form of obedience. But this is only a phase, only one stop on a longer journey. Finally the day came when the humble tops of the wooden churches of Solovetskii Island arose from the waves of the icy sea and came into the sight of young Fedor.

More than one hundred years had passed since

Herman of Tot'ma, an anchorite from the Karelian shore of the White Sea, and Savvatii, a monk from the Kirillov-Belozersk Monastery who had also been in Valaam, erected a cross on the uninhabited island and began their ascetical life there (1429). At that time they had no disciples. St. Savvatii did not die on the island but on the mainland. He was buried in a chapel on the Vyg river on September 27, 1435. Herman, unable to bear the loneliness and the difficulty of obtaining food on Solovki, also left the island. However, in a year he returned together with a new anchorite, a Novgorodian by birth from Lake Onega — St. Zosima. It was St. Zosima who was the true founder of the Solovetskii Monastery. St. Herman, who is locally revered in Solovki, did not leave the monastery his name. Through his enthusiastic stories about the ocean hermitage, St. Herman was the first to be able to attract new persons to come to the island. But he himself had to leave the island more than once for a less severe climate. Although St. Herman outlived St. Zosima, he never became the hegumen of the hermitage which he too helped to establish with his labors. He also did not end his days on the island.

St. Zosima was not only a courageous ascetic who was victorious over hunger, cold, and demonic temptations but he was also the elder of the monks, a zealous master and the organizer of the community. He built a church on the spot where he had experienced a vision of a bright church descending from heaven and he named this church "The Transfiguration." The Russian north liked to dedicate its humble wooden churches to the mysterious, spiritual Transfiguration. The cold and gloom of the northern elements were, it seemed, overcome by the fire and light of the Transfiguration. The severity of ascetical labors was illumined by the promise of triumph — of undecaying, imperishable holy flesh. One of the chapels of the Solovetskii church was dedicated to St. Nikolai, the miracle-worker, the ruler of the ocean deep. From the charter given by Novgorod "to the house of Our Saviour, his Holy Mother, and Saint Nikolai," we can presume that another chapel or church was dedicated to the Holy Mother of God. In a few years, still under St. Zosima, a large, but still wooden, church of the Transfiguration replaced the little one. This larger church of the Transfiguration then had the church of the Assumption built on to its east side. Thus, on a wild island in the middle of the polar sea, Holy Russia appears with names of its favorite holy events and with symbols of its inner divine reflection (a spiritual reflection not expressed in books but through experience).

The origin of both founders of the Solovetskii Monastery already points to the two roads leading from Rus' to the White Sea — one from the Moscow south; another from the Novgorod south-west. It is likely that among the original monks we could have met natives from both Great Russian governments, with a numerical majority of Novgorodians. The local Finno-Karelians began to join the Russians rather early. They came to the monastery while St. Zosima was still alive, were baptized, and sometimes they were tonsured as monks.

At that time the whole northern coast was drawn toward 'Great' Novgorod. The slaves and peasants of the Novgorod boyars hacked out their settlements among the sparse native population of Karelians and Samoeds. They opened up small islands of fertile land for their masters and engaged in hunting, and in the fishing and salt trade. Together with the stewards of the Novgorod merchants, hermits and colonies of monks from southern monasteries penetrated the north, serving the religious needs of Russian settlers. Frequently the monastic hermitage served as the parish church for an extensive district.

At the time of the founding of the Solovetskii Monastery, there were no significant monasteries within a hundred versts. The Solovetskii pioneers anticipated the natural flow of the colonization movement and created the only significant center in the entire Orthodox north.

The Solovetskii Island is totally devoid of fertile land. Its surface consists of cliffs, lakes, and hills overgrown with forests. Its climate is not as severe as might be expected by its geographical latitude. The sea, which — except for the coastal strip — does not freeze, tempers the winter cold. Frosts are rarely overly bitter. But the land there is incapable of feeding its inhabitants. This made it necessary to depend on the mainland for trade and for suitable soil. While St. Zosima was still alive, the monastery directed its activity along these two lines. His *Life* describes the monastic economy in the following way: "Much wood was cut and prepared and water was taken from the sea. Salt was produced and sold to traders. From these traders all kinds of essential goods were obtained for the monastery. They labored at other trades too and also fished. . . And thus, by their labor and by the sweat of their brow, they fed themselves. . ." But at an early stage in the life of the Solovetskii Monastery, the boyars of Novgorod were giving the monastery arable lands along the coast of the White Sea. The oldest of the documents which has come down to us belongs to the famous Marfa Boretskaia, the widow of the "governor" [*posadnik*], Isak Andreevich. The boyarina and her son Fedor granted the monastery "two fields by the sea and the Suma river, by the chapel where Parfenka and Pershitsa live; and in that land, the hamlets, the harvests, woods and field, and the forest lakes." These lands were to be "forever possessed by the hegumen and the elders, and my husband Isak, my parents and my children should be prayed for. And let them celebrate Dimitrii's day."

The relationship between the monastery and the Novgorod settlers was not always peaceful. Quite early, hunters and fishermen, Russians as well as Karelians, stopped at the Solovetskii Island and began to offend the monks. The monastery, positioned in a desolate spot on the empty sea, inevitably came under the authority of 'Great' Novgorod. It was to Novgorod that the monastery had to turn in order to seek help against its oppressors. And it found it. A document has been preserved with the seals of Novgorod's archbishop Iona, Novgorod's "governor" [*posadnik*], its "lieutenant-governor" [*tysiatskii*], and the elders of Novgorod's five districts. This document recognizes the right of the Solovetskii Monastery to rule "from the ocean" over the whole group of islands — Solovki, Anzery, the Muksalms (Greater and Lesser), the Zaiatskiis (Greater and Lesser), "and the smaller islands." "And neither the boyars of Novgorod, the Karelians, nor anyone else is to enter upon these islands . . . Whoever comes to these islands to hunt or for gain or to procure lard or leather — each must pay a tithe to the house of the Holy Saviour and St. Nikolai and this tithe will be calculated from every possession." Anyone who disobeys "will give 'Great Novgorod' one-hundred rubles as a penalty" (comparable to about 8,000 rubles in the nineteenth century.)

Dependent on Novgorod in its economic and civil affairs, the Solovetskii Monastery was all the more dependent on it in ecclesiastical matters. It fell under the extensive diocese of the archbishop of Novgorod and this dependence was canonical. But we are surprised perhaps by the strict forms in which this dependence was originally expressed. All of the first priors of the monastery were Novgorod monks, sent to Solovki from Novgorod, i.e. they were not chosen from among the members of the brethren. The newcomers, however, could not long endure the severity of the northern "Thebaid" and, having forsaken their flock, returned to Novgorod. They did, however, accomplish much good for Solovki by petitioning on its behalf before the city leaders. But the spiritual fathers of the monastery remained its founders, St. Herman and St. Zosima. Finally, the inhabitants of Solovki began to solicit persistently for a hegumen from among their midst. Archbishop Iona of Novgorod finally agreed that their request was fair. The brethren chose the monk Zosima and Archbishop Iona, after first summoning Zosima to Novgorod, approved him as the fourth hegumen of the Solovetskii Monastery. Later, when the Solovetskii vestry became quite rich, one of its greatest treasures was the humble chasuble of white linen (only the part covering the shoulder was of silk) which the archbishop gave to St. Zosima upon his appointment as hegumen. According to ancient tradition, the priors served in this chasuble on the day which commemorated St. Zosima.

During St. Zosima's leadership, there was intense work on the rebuilding of the church, cells, and official buildings. The regulation of church services and the monastic "cell" rule were finalized. St. Zosima's rule, preserved in the monastery's library, was composed in accordance with the Jerusalem *Typikon*. Revering the memory of his predecessor, St. Zosima transferred the relics of St. Savvatii from the chapel in Vyg where the saint had died to the island. There were already miracles reported by his grave. The prior of the Kirillov-Belozersk Monastery, where the respected *starets* had begun his feats, wrote to the hegumen of the Solovetskii Monastery convincing him not to deprive himself of the healing power of the relics of St. Savvatii. His relics were then solemnly buried in the monastery behind the altar of the Church of the Assumption. Above the grave an icon was placed, the first one painted by Ivan of Novgorod who knew the *starets* personally and who witnessed his death. Among his economic labors, Zosima had to undertake a second trip to Novgorod to seek justice, a situation caused by the violence of the boyars' men. In Novgorod this time he was coldly received by Marfa, the former benefactress of the monastery. The *posadnitsa* Marfa, whose people had offended the monks of Solovki, chased him disrespectfully from the court. It was then, it is told, that he predicted the fate awaiting the proud city: "The days are coming when the dwellers of this house will not step upon this court, and the doors of this house will close . . . and this court will be empty." The proximity of the great catastrophe also casts its shadow onto another ominous vision related in Zosima's *Life*. Marfa, who repented, invited the hegumen to a feast. During the feast, the saint had a strange vision: six of the feasting guests, who were among the most famous boyars, were sitting headless. Zosima could not refrain from tears. In one year, the saint's vision came to pass: six heads came off by order of the Grand Prince Ivan Vasil'evich after the battle of Shelonsk. The saint returned to the island with a new charter from Marfa Boretskaia (written by her son in 1470) for new lands.

As he was dying in 1478, the builder of the Solovetskii Monastery blessed the brethren and promised a glorious future for the monastery: "I am leaving you in body, but I will constantly be with you in spirit. And let this be known to you: if, upon my death, God blesses me, then this monastery will grow even more and then many brothers will gather in spiritual love. And this holy house will have an abundance of all spiritual goods and there will be no scarcity of those needs essential for sustaining the flesh." These last words describe quite well the spirit of this northern monastery during all five hundred years of its glorious history. It was able to combine extensive economic activity with a tradition of spiritual life which did not decay, even though, externally surrounding it, there was a period of decline. Enormous possession did not stifle the spiritual calling of the monastery. The significance of the labors of the Solovetskii Monastery lies not in severe asceticism nor in mystical contemplation but in a sensible merging of the active and the contemplative life, in the combination of work and prayer.

After the death of the great founder, eighteen priors replaced each other until the time of hegumen Aleksei, under whom Fedor Kolychov was tonsured. We do not have much knowledge of the events which occurred during the relatively short terms of these other priors. The monastery did, however, continue to grow and its wealth increased, even though such wealth was somewhat undermined by fires in 1485 and 1538. Even the fall of Novgorod had no effect on the monastery's economic prosperity. Ivan III granted the monastery a charter which permitted it to rule over the surrounding islands. The charter was confirmed by his son. The archbishops of Novgorod continued to make contributions to the monastery and grant it privileged, "tax free" charters. Zosima's third successor, hegumen Dosifei, compiled a life of the holy founders, Zosima and Savvatii. Although it underwent rhetorical treatment by Metropolitan Spiridon in 1503 at the request of the humble author, it paints, if not the spiritual image of the saints, then the spiritual atmosphere of life in the monastery in rather rich and concrete strokes. Five years after the death of Herman, Isaiia, the hegumen at that time, had Herman's coffin moved and placed by the altar next to the relics of St. Savvatii.

In 1514, at the command of the Grand Prince, the monastery was inspected and officially recorded by the Moscow secretaries [*d'iaki*]. Some traces of certain interference by the Moscow rulers into the internal life of the monastery have been retained in the cadaster [*pistsovaia kniga*]. Hegumen Evfimii, mentioned in the official description of the monastery, was, for some reason, relieved from duties. The officials ordered four elders to head the monastery temporarily "until the Grand Prince gave them a new hegumen, or permitted [Evfimii] to reassume the position." The dependence of a Solovetskii hegumen's confirmation on Moscow's consent might date from this time. This, however, did not negate the rights of the archbishop of Novgorod, under whose jurisdiction the monastery continued to be, just as it was before.

In any case, hegumen Aleksei (Iurenev) assumed the leadership of the Solovetskii Monastery in 1534, according to the official record of the Moscow secretaries and according to a document of Grand Prince Ivan Vasil'evich (the Terrible). In Filipp's years as a monk, the young Tsar (or his government) appears as the monastery's benefactor. After the fire of 1538, the Tsar recompensed the monastery with a series of coastal villages with salt works and an annual tax sum. In 1541 he granted the monastery a "privileged" charter (a confirmation of Vasilii III's charter), according to which the monastery's monks and peasants were freed from civil jurisdiction, "[whose] domain was open robbery and brigandage." Jurisdiction over all dependent people was transferred to the hegumen. Now not even the archbishop of Novgorod could interfere with the non-spiritual affairs of the monastery. While preparing for the Kazan' campaign, the sovereign wrote to Solovki through his boyars requesting prayers for victory. In this case, he ordered that the monks be given generous alms ("seven *rubles* and eight Moscow *dengi*").

From the time of Ivan the Terrible, Moscow does not forget this northern monastery, intending — it seems — to replace the former generosity of the now impoverished Novgorod.

About the time of the second Solovetskii fire in 1538, a thirty year old man from Onega came to hegumen Aleksei and asked to be accepted as a novice. Fedor did not wish to disclose his wordly name, probably for the sake of humility rather than for safety from the Moscow rulers. He went through the typical severe monastic routine of labor: "chopping wood, digging in the garden, moving stones, and carrying packs and manure on his shoulders." He worked in the garden, clearing and fertilizing the poor, rocky soil. He had to bear even more difficult ordeals for his humility, taking "much deprecation and abuse from those who were unreasonable." He did not become angry and bore everything meekly. After a year and a half he was tonsured and named Filipp. But the "angelic image" did not abrogate his heavy labors. Filipp first bore his obedience in the kitchen, then in the bakery. He chopped wood, carried water, and heated the stove. During these years, he was under the spiritual guidance of hieromonk Iona, "a marvelous *starets* who in his youth was a disciple of St. Aleksandr Svirskii," already renouned at that time. Iona taught Filipp all the monastic and ecclesiastical rules until his disciple, having excelled in liturgical knowledge was appointed "ecclesiarch" — the monk whose task was to supervise the liturgical ritual. It is related that *starets* Iona foretold that Filipp "will become the prior of our holy house." Did he have a presentiment of the lofty and fearful destiny awaiting Filipp? Up to now, under the parvis of the Church of Saints Zosima and Savvatii, next to Metropolitan Filipp's tombstone, the memorial plate of his teacher has also been preserved: "In the summer of 7076 (1568) the servant of God, Iona Shamin, passed away in the month of January on the tenth day." *Starets* Iona entered eternity only two years earlier than his spiritual son.

But the Solovetskii rules of work did not suppress Filipp's thirst for the spiritual life. It is during these years that Filipp's withdrawal to the forest occurs: "There, having raised his mind to God, he practiced prayer." The anchorite spent "not a few years" in this seclusion. Then he returned to his usual labors. Let us remember this valuable detail of his biography, so scanty in personal characteristics. This biographical detail, along with Filipp's earlier work as a shepherd, tends to underscore the real motive of his becoming a monk — that is, a spiritual and not a secular motive.

After ten years of life at the Solovetskii Monastery, Filipp was in the forefront of all the monks in both talent and accomplishment. Hegumen Aleksei liked him and already saw in him his possible successor. Was Filipp's origin — was his worldly wealth — known in Solovki at this time? It is possible that at least the prior and Filipp's spiritual father knew such facts. In any case, Kolychov's name was certainly disclosed in Novgorod when he was approved as hegumen. It may be thought that the name "Kolychov," together with the personal qualities of Fedor, caused Aleksei to settle on him as his choice to succeed him as hegumen. Depressed by old age and illnesses, Aleksei decided, while still alive, to remove the burden of rule from himself and place it on young shoulders. Despite Filipp's refusals, and citing his own infirmity, the hegumen offered the monks the chance to elect a new hegumen. The unanimous choice fell on Filipp. And Filipp did not contradict them.

With the old hegumen's letter, and accompanied by several monks, Filipp left for Novgorod to be con-

firmed. It was spring when the men from Solovki set out
on the long journey to Novgorod, travelling through lake
and swamp so they could return to the islands before the
winter ice set in. Archbishop Feodosii received the monks
who brought the hegumen's letter, but he did not see
Filipp among them. "Where is the chosen one?" he asked.
The chosen one had hidden out of humility. Having
finally come before the archbishop and having satisfied
him with wise replies to his penetrating questions, Filipp
was ordained a priest and received the hegumen's staff
from the hands of the archbishop. " 'Here is your father',
said Feodosii, 'keep him in Christ's image and listen to
him in all things'."

While in Novgorod, Filipp had to renew familial
ties and old friendships. He also had to assume possession
of the properties he once left. Already a rich man, he
returned to Solovki to use his fortune for the further
building and enhancement of the monastery. The Moscow
runaway had once sought humble poverty. Filipp the
hegumen was not a "non-possessor" in the sense that the
Trans Volga elders understood "non-possession."

In the middle of August he was met at the monastery with crosses, icons, and the ringing of church bells.
The former hegumen and the brethren came to the shore
to meet him and to accompany him to the hegumen's
place in the church. Filipp arrived just in time for the
ecclesiastical holy day of the Assumption. On August
17, 1548, he celebrated his first liturgy in the monastery
and gave his first sermon.

Here Filipp's *Life* enters a strange episode. Unfortunately, in its sparing account it does not clarify the
episode. To our surprise, the hegumen so triumphantly
ordained, does not remain in the monastery and relin-
quishes the responsibility of ruling. The *Life* records the
following:

The saint, though accepting the elder's position, does not change his former way. Reaching for the ascetic more than before and subjecting himself to yet greater physical labors, he saw himself praised and respected. Adorned with humility from youth, Filipp attributed it all to vanity. Because of this he left the hegumen's chair and again went into the wilderness, coming to the monastery only to receive the Eucharist, the Holy Body and Blood of Christ our Lord. During this time, the former hegumen who had tonsured him was in charge — for a year and a half — until he passed away. And then Filipp was again appointed.

This case, surprising in itself, of the renunciation by the just elected hegumen becomes even more surprising if we turn our attention to another fact. In order for the aged Aleksei to resume his duties as hegumen and in order for Filipp to be confirmed as hegumen for a second time, new trips to Novgorod were demanded. Archbishop Feodosii had to appoint hegumens to Solovki three times in the course of two years. The election of Filipp as hegumen for a second time took place upon Aleksei's death at a meeting of the monks. This corresponded to a formal appointment. All this points to the fact that, in leaving for the wilderness, Filipp had truly abdicated. His anchorite existence was not merely caused by a prolonged ascetical isolation. Something happened in Solovki, something which temporarily changed Filipp's decision. We can only guess at the motives for his leaving his post as hegumen, a decision which caused so much trouble for the monastery.

Two possibilities present themselves. From the very beginning of his rule as hegumen, Filipp may have clashed with a faction opposed to him, a faction capable of instigating the former hegumen against him (or at least of setting the former hegumen at odds with him). If so, then we have in this episode the embryo of that conflict which revealed itself twenty years later, when, during the trial of the metropolitan, a group of Solovetskii monks testified against their former hegumen. The *Life*, compiled in Solovki, could have evaded the page of internal discord which was obviously unpleasant for the monastery.

But the inner motivation suggested by the *Life* can also be accepted as convincing. In this case, Filipp removes the burden of rule from himself because of ascetical apprehensions. He doubts his powers, repents of his former assent, and flees from his position of rule. In both cases we have before us a not overly strong character, an unambitious person who knew the measure of his powers and responsibilities. His nature was a more timid one, striving to evade power in humble recognition of his own weakness. Whether Filipp runs from himself or from his enemies, he still *runs*. We have seen the boyar son as a runaway. We have seen not a fighter, but a fugitive. And this is how we must remember him, lest we allow the image of the practical hegumen and the courageous confessor to becloud Filipp's basic nature — that meek and humble "weakness" in which "the power of God is perfected." (II Corinthians 12:9).

If Filipp the monk fled from the position of rule because of a lack of confidence in his own powers, then these powers were found in him in abundance when the time and burden of rule ultimately fell upon him. In his new rank Filipp discovered rare administrative talents. The eighteen years of his position as hegumen were an era in the life of the Solovetskii Monastery. He is justifiably considered to be the monastery's second founder. Until recent times the Solovetskii churches, buildings, workshops, lakes, and hermitages have preserved the memory of the tireless activity of the holy hegumen.

The enduring memory and also preserved documents compensate partially for the gaps in the *Life*, which is particularly scanty in the presentation of these years. Actually, the very character of our sources creates a certain onesidedness of information. We know Filipp the master and the administrator well. But we do not know at all the spiritual father of the monastery and we know almost nothing of his own personal religious life. In these years Filipp presents to us a difficult side of himself, a side which, of course, is not the most important one in the make-up of his spiritual strengths, but something quite characteristic of ancient Russian monasticism, and in part, of this northern monastery. In becoming acquainted with it, we turn one of the most remarkable pages of Russian Church culture.

As hegumen, Filipp is, above all, the builder, the establisher of the monastery. We do not know the degree to which the monastery was restored under hegumen Aleksei after the fire of 1538. Services, in any case, were held in the churches. It was Filipp who decided to change the wooden buildings to stone. He began with the Cathedral of the Assumption of the Mother of God. Novgorodian masters began the masonary work in 1552 and after five years, on the feastday of the Assumption in 1557, the cathedral was consecrated. Upstairs a chapel was dedicated to the forerunner — St. John the Baptist, the Tsar's patron saint. Under the church were the bread baking kitchens. A huge refectory and a large storeroom were added to the side. Above the refectory rose a belfry with a clock which chimed every hour.

After one year (1558) Filipp laid the foundations for the Cathedral of the Transfiguration which in size and beauty was to surpass the Church of the Assumption. The brethren who had joyfully greeted the commencement of the building, now became disturbed at the hegumen's bravery. "Father," they said, "there is not enough in the treasury and we are in great poverty, for there are no surrounding towns. From where will you get money to build a great church?" Means were found. The Tsar also helped much. Without sparing his own money, the hegumen himself decorated the new church with icons, vessels, chasubles, candleholders, and icon lamps. In the northern side of this church he chose his burial place. Filipp wanted his memory to be commemorated along with prayers for his parents and he provided generous contributions for this. The *Solovetskii Chronicle* contains the following: "Filipp Stefanovich Kolychov, the hegumen of the Solovetskii Monastery, asked all the brethren to include the "eternal memory" for him in the litany [*litiia*] and he asked Father Stefan, and his mother, the nun Varsonofiia, and his brother Boris, to write his name into the litany [*litiia*] when he passed away and also to celebrate his memory in November on the seventh day. And he gave a *dacha* and 171 rubles to the monastery, in addition to other *dachas* . . ."

Filipp was not able to personally consecrate the Cathedral of the Transfiguration, something which was dear to him. The cathedral was consecrated on August 6, 1566 when its founder had just been appointed to the metropolitanate of Moscow. The Cathedral of the Transfiguration, like that of the Assumption, was built on solid foundations and its arches were supported by two enormous pillars. From the outside, the tall, pillar-like church had the look of a fortress stronghold. It was crowned by five cupolas, already common to Muscovite style; the middle cupola, however, was unusually large and was crowned with a Novgorodian headpiece. There were six chapels in the church. On the sides of the main altar were the chapels of the Archangels and the Solovetskii miracle-workers. In the cupolas of the Cathedral were four small chapels of the Twelve and Seventy apostles, and the angels of the Tsar's children, Ioann Lestvichnik and Feodor Stratilat.

Filipp's building was not limited to the cathedral churches. He constructed stone buildings for cells, a hospital for monks and pilgrims, "hermitages" in the forests, a small secluded monastery or *skit* on the Zaiiatskii Island where he also built "a ward," a kitchen, and a stone pier. Zaiiatskii Island served as a station for ships which were held up by head winds on the way to Solovki. In the Solovetskii harbor itself Filipp poured mounds upon which he put tall crosses which served as beacons for the seafarers. It was also under Filipp's direction that the monastery houses in Novgorod and Vologda were built. Instead of the old stone hammers and gongs, copper bells were cast for the new churches. Three of these copper bells have been preserved. They weigh about 6,250 pounds, 2,880 pounds, and 1,080 pounds. The largest one is called "the Saint's" in memory of Filipp. Inscriptions on these bells list the names of the Tsars, the hierarchs, donors, hegumens, and also the masters who cast the copper bells. All the bells were cast in "the famed and glorious city of Pskov."

The passion for building frequently appears as a noble form of extravagance which ruins the community with splendid, though not economical, undertakings. For the hegumen of the Solovetskii Monastery, care for his children came first. His precepts to his brethren have not been preserved. The rule which was in effect during his time as hegumen has also not come down to us. But in its basic characteristics the rule existing during Filipp's time was probably the one preserved from the time of Zosima. A portion of the rule, however, has been pre-served — the book compiled by Filipp in 1553 about the clothing of monks. Clothing and provisions for all

the brethren presented problems to the hegumen. We
know from Metropolitan Filipp's epistle to Solovki (see
the Appendix) that there were two hundred monks. In
addition to the monks, there were many "working people"
in Solovki. This same epistle determines the number of
"working people" to be three hundred. All of them "ate,
drank, and they wore monastic clothing." The same, but
to a greater degree, applies to those who had taken monastic vows. Ancient Russia knew three types of monastic
communities. Predominating were the "private" ["*osob-
nyi*"] monasteries which retained private property and
even separate tables. Solovki was a strict cenobitic monastery excluding private economy. In the ancient *Typikon* of the Solovetskii Monastery their custom is described in the following way: "The hegumen and the priests
and the cathedral elders and all the monks eat and drink in
the refectory. Food is the same for everyone and it is not
taken into the cells unless a monk is sick. Food and drink
cannot be taken out of the refectory. All clothing and
foot gear are given to everyone from the treasury." St.
Filipp was not an admirer of excessive asceticism. He
improved both the monastic food and clothing and demanded tireless labor to accomplish this. He did not
tolerate idlers and accepted into the monastery only
those who, like him, were ready to eat by the sweat of
their brow, as stipulated in the apostle's words: "If any
one will not work, let him not eat." (II Thessalonians
3:10).

The meager Solovetskii gardens, in which Filipp
had worked when he was a novice, could not feed the
brethren. Filipp began, or more accurately, increased
the dairy economy. One obstacle was Zosima's *Testament*
which (in accordance with the *Studite Rule*) forbade
the breeding of procreating animals near the cloister.
With the permission of the Archbishop of Novgorod,

Filipp partially changed St. Zosima's *Rule*. On one of the islands, the Muksal'mskii, he started a large cattle yard. He also let a herd of reindeer into the Solovetskii forests. The cattle yard produced fertilizer but demanded hay. The forests were cleared for hayfields. The forest was cut for other reasons as well: for wood for the brick works which prepared building materials. To save the forest from wasteful destruction, Filipp made sure of proper timber felling. Openings appeared in the forests; a network of roads cut the island in all directions. Simultaneously, the draining of swamps by means of canals and dams took place. One is most amazed by Filipp's hydro-technical work.

According to the calculation of hegumen Dosifei in 1836, Solovetskii Island (which is 25 by 16 *versts*) has 97 lakes with specific names excluding the small, nameless lakes. Right near the monastery there is the large Holy Lake (700 by 200 *sazhens*). In ancient times no pilgrims entered the monastery without having bathed or washed in its holy waters. Twice a year the water in the lake was blessed and the sick were healed. This lake is an artificial reservoir which was dug at the request of hegumen Filipp. By means of a whole network of canals, he brought in water from fifty-two lakes. For drainage he dug two other canals to the sea, one of which passes right under the monastery. It is not known, of course, whether this water system existed in the same form during St. Filipp's time. It was probably extended later. From Moscow, from the metropolitanate, the saint wrote to Solovki in 1568 about continuing the project of digging out a pond. Filipp, however, was able to build a mill for grinding grain on the canal which was within the boundaries of the monastery. (Prior to this, the mills were three *versts* from the monastery). The "Solovetskii Chronicler" even ascribes the invention of some kind of machines or implements to St. Filipp. Besides the mill, Filipp started workshops for making fur and shoe materials from the skin of their own reindeer. Skillful engravers worked on items for church use, items made from "fish tooth," i.e. walrus bone. This art always flourished in Solovki, from where it spread to the whole northern littoral. Its origin pre-dates Filipp's time as hegumen. Until rather recent times, the altar cross in the Church of the Assumption was made from walrus teeth with carved representations of the Crucifixion and of saints. This cross, together with a carved *Deisus*, is mentioned as early as 1514 in a description of the monastery.

Nevertheless all this manufacturing activity in Solovki could not feed its inhabitants. Because of natural conditions, the island could not become self-sufficient economically. Solovki was only the center of a broad patrimonial economy whose body spread over all the western coastal region, including parts of inner Russia as well. By Filipp's time, the Solovetskii Monastery was the largest landowner in the Russian north. It clashes only occasionally with the wave of colonization which came from the Kirillo-Belozersk Monastery. By means of contributions and purchases, the possessions of the old Novgorod boyars and a significant segment of government lands, which were developed by free colonizers, gradually came into the hands of the Solovetskii Monastery. It is not without interest to take a cursory look at the size and character of the Solovetskii patrimonial economy which, precisely under hegumen Filipp, was subjected to administrative regulations.

The monastery's possessions, as those previously of the Novgorod boyars, were not continuous territories but were scattered island-like throughout the swampy and wooded wilderness. The ·settlers' homesteads arose quite naturally along the shores of the many "ocean" rivers flowing into the White Sea, and along the coast of the sea itself. Because of the very nature of this country, these settlements were primarily commercial: hunting, fishing, and salt works. The documents [*gramoty*] are full of regulations about "net-fishing places [*toni*] and the fish catch, the tillable forest and the productive lakes"; and the second most mentioned topic in the regulations concerns "arable land" [*"stradomaia"* or *"oramaia" zemlia*]. The villages had few people. Sometimes they consisted of one or two households which were similar to farmsteads. An agricultural family under the protection of a rich owner of a patrimonial estate [*votchinnik*], perhaps with the help of the latter's capital, i.e. implements and loans of provisions, waged a one on one fight against the severe, but potentially "tillable" nature which surrounded them. Among the settlers different groups can be distinguished: peasants, cotters [*bobyli*], and cossacks. The latter represented a nomadic, non-permanent group of hired hands living on someone else's land. But they were all personally free and always at liberty to leave the monastic land if they wished to leave "because of sins." They first, however, had to clear up their debts and obligations [*tiaglo*]. These settlements were mostly grouped in regions primarily connected by rivers: the Suma, the Virma, and the Shizhnia, etc. . . . . All these small rivers flow along the Karelian and the littoral, i.e. the western shore of the White Sea. During the course of the sixteenth century, the monastic possessions move eastward toward Onega, but do not, however, reach this river. Separate parts of this economy in the sixteenth century were the few patrimonies in the districts of Dvinsk and Kargopol'sk, even in Bezhetsk (more recently the province of Tver) where in the 1560's the boyar Ivan Vasil'evich Polev relinquished his patrimony to the Solovetskii Monastery.

The fragmentary documents of the Solovetskii archive which have come down to us do not make it possible to compile a complete picture of the Solovetskii possessions or to sum them up in numbers. The fate of some of the regions, accidentally known to us, is evidence of the strong economic growth at the end of the fifteenth and sixteenth centuries. In general, according to Kliuchevskii's observation, the Solovetskii Monastery discovered "a striving to introduce their activity in a wilderness which others refused to exploit." In other words, the monastery displayed agricultural initiative. It not only fed off the land, it also fed the dependent population. The Solovetskii Monastery was the active cultural center in the region.

From the time of Filipp's position as hegumen, we have three "administrative charters" ["*ustavnyi gramoty*"] given by him to the Solovetskii patrimonial population and representing the codification of the patrimonial law then in effect. Leaving aside the charter of 1561 to the peasants of the village of Puzyrev in Upper Bezhetsk whose mode of life differed greatly from that of coastal villages, we have the charter of 1548 to five regions headed by Virma. We also have the charter of 1564 to the Sumskii region. It is difficult to say what in this charter should be ascribed to ancient custom and what to the hegumen's initiative. The earliest charter, dated August 17, 1548, — the very day of Filipp's assumption of the duties of hegumen — can least serve as evidence of the hegumen's initiative. The primary content of the administrative charter of 1548 is the fixing of the financial obligations of various categories of monastic people, obligations going for the maintenance of the patrimonial administration. The general tendency is a defense of the peasantry against arbitrary administrative requisitions: "From the bail nothing is to be given to anyone." "They give nothing," "nothing is to be taken" runs through the whole charter. The monastery, possessing the right to judge its peasants in litigations with strangers (and in cases of serious crime), defends them in the court of the Tsar's rural district administrator [*volostel'*] in Vygozer. The constable [*dovodchik*] had to accompany the litigants to the district court "and had to defend the peasant energetically in court and he must not take any gifts from the peasant on the way." The conclusion is especially characteristic: "If our elder, commissioner, or constable harms in any way his peasant or cossack, or if [they] take anything not specified by the *gramota*, then the guilty ones must show that they are humble and still capable of holding office and those whom they have harmed will be compensated; we will order them to be reimbursed two-fold."

The monastic economy, of course, was not a philanthropic establishment. It vigilantly looked after its interests, guarding its interests especially from the ever transient "cossack" population which, by its very non-permanent nature, lent itself poorly to accountability. The monastery demanded that each settler declare to the government each "unknown cossack" living on his land. Each settler also had to take note of the departure of any cossack. The declaration of the presence and the departure of cossacks was accompanied by a payment of a tax.

The strict measures against drunkenness and playing dice [*zern'*] reveal both the strictness of zealous masters and the supervision of morality by spiritual rulers: "Those peasants and cossacks who play dice must pay the monastery a half ruble, the town commissioner [*prikazshchik*] ten *altyny*, and the constable [*dovodchik*] two *grivny*. The players are to be chased out of the region." This fine, enormous for its time, was doubled for drinkers of wine and winemakers, though without the threat of exile. "Those traders [*torgovye liudi*] who travel through regional districts [*volosti*] in winter and summer to sell wine are not to be received by the town commissioner and wine is not to be bought from them by the town commissioner, the peasants, the cossacks, and they are not to make their own wine." In order to evaluate fully the reason for this severity, we must keep in mind that, according to tradition, St. Zosima completely forbade the use of wine in the monastery and this prohibition was extended to the monastic peasants.

The administrative charter [*ustavnaia gramota*] of 1564 to the Sumskii region already has the unmistakable stamp of hegumen Filipp's personal activity. It introduces reforms and consolidates other reforms which took place previously. In 1548, five regions are administered from one center — from Virma. The structure of the administration is not complicated: the elder commissioner [*starets prikazchik*], the treasurer [*kelar'*], and the constable [*dovodchik*] (the court bailiff [*sudebnyi pristav*]) seemingly constitute the whole administrative personnel. In the charter of 1564 we already see three administrative centers. There are commissioners [*prikazchiki*] in Virma and Kolezhma (probably with subordinate officials). There are minor police officials [*desiatskie*] in each region [*volost'*]; and in Suma there was a chief administrator [*starosta*] in charge of everyone, in addition to the agent of the prince [*tiun*] and a police herald [*biriuch*]. The other reform, which is actually sanctioned by the charter of 1564, consists of a new form of taxation. We know about the population's dissatisfaction with the old, arbitrary system of "splitting" [*"razrub"*], i. e. the apportionment of tax or fiscal obligations. From this time, the tax apportionments are made not by the patrimonial authority but by officials elected by the people: two each from the "wealthy," from the "moderately" well-off, from the "poor" peasants, and from the "cossacks." Here we observe the beginning of that self-government on monastic lands which had already long prevailed for boyar peasants in the north: from that time the Novgorod boyars were "depleted" and their former slaves [*kholopy*] and "courtiers" [*"dvoriane"*] became "State orphans" [*"gosudarevy siroty"*], i.e. free State peasants. At the same time, this phenomenon cannot but be compared with the policy of self-rule and self-imposed taxation by city and district communities [*miry*], a policy which was introduced in the first half of the reign of Ivan the Terrible.

Two of the specific articles of the Sumskii charter are especially interesting. One of them attempts to bring youths under taxation: "And those peasants' children and nephews, who will in time hunt for game and birds, catch fish, and pick berries and mushrooms, should be, in the same way as the cossacks, taxed according to worth." The other article deals with the production of salt by the peasants: "In all our villages salt was cooked for 160 days through summer and winter in large iron pans [*tsreny*]. For winter and summer cooking, six hundred *sazheni* of wood were necessary for each iron pan each year. Wood may be stocked for one year, but not for following years. Whoever shall cook extra days and cut extra wood shall be fined and the extra salt and wood will be taken to the monastery." In all probability, this limitation on the peasants' salt production had the goal of ensuring the interests of patrimonial industry.

From the contents of the separate articles of administrative charters we can see that agricultural interests were not in the forefront. The poor northern soil produces little grain, and then only oats and barley. Only trade with the grain producing southern areas could feed the local population. The main item of this trade was salt. Hence, the production of salt was almost the main source of Solovetskii wealth. The production of and trade in salt was, to a large degree, concentrated in the hands of the monastery. Each year caravans of boats went up the Dvina to Kholmogorsk, Ustiug Velikii, and Tot'ma, right up to Vologda, and returned loaded with grain. Vologda attained significance as the most important storage point in trade between "the South" and "the Coast." The settlement built by St. Filipp in Vologda had to serve both the commissioner and the monastic laborers who were occupied with the salt trade. The following figures give an idea of the scope of this trade. In the middle of the sixteenth century the monastery sold 6,000 to 10,000 *pudy* of salt; in the middle of the seventeenth century, 130,000. At the end of the sixteenth century the monastery bought up to 20 *pudy* of wax and up to 8,000 *chetverti* (56,000 *pudy*) of rye. This quantity shows that the monastery fed not only hundreds of its monks and workers but thousands of peasants as well. We have information, relating directly to Filipp's time, that, in addition to bread and wax, leather and cloth were brought to the monastery. In a word, what looms before us is a picture of a centralized economy. The Solovetskii patrimony is not a series of small peasant economies united only in the goal of exploitation as Professor S. F. Platonov pictured the old boyar patrimonies of Novgorod. If production was rather small and agricultural, then it was nevertheless built upon capitalistic foundations. This is not a simple "feeding off" the land, a direct extraction of the soil's riches. Trade, and furthermore, a distant trade, an organized and planned trade, was the lifeblood of the patrimonial organism. The monetary form of all the obligations of the monastic population is related to this and excludes all notions of a "natural" economy. But if the monastery externally appears with capitalistic traits, then within its own possessions it retains all the characteristics of the patrimonial *votchinnik*. It introduces moral ideas in relationship to the dependent population. For the monastery, the population is not an object of exploitation but rather the center of fatherly guardianship and upbringing.

This entire system not only fell on the shoulders of hegumen Filipp but, to a significant degree, is his creation. The great increase in the monastery's possessions and the codification of patrimonial law which it brought about occurs precisely in his time. St. Filipp, who once rejected the burdens of rule, grew in a few years into a model administrator who reveals to us a new side of his personality. Were he living at the end of the sixteenth century, he would have had to combine his administrative qualities with the talents of a strategist or at least a military engineer. But the defense of Solovki from the "cursed Germans," i.e. the Swedes, begins only in the 1570's. The monastery was enclosed by its Cyclopean walls of rough stone only under Fedor Ivanovich (1584-1594). From the end of the sixteenth century Solovki is already a first class stronghold defending the northern boundaries of the Muscovite government. Fortunately, under hegumen Filipp, the turbulent forces of the *strel'tsy* and the artillery men did not trouble the quiet of the cells with the possible beginning of the corruption of established cenobitic life. Nothing violated the monastery's strict work discipline and its prayerful silence.

Unfortunately we know far less of hegumen Filipp's spiritual accomplishments than we do of his economic undertakings. But this accidental circumstance should not distort his image. We should end our description of Filipp's Solovetskii years with some information characterizing his religious attitude. It is true that part of the information

relates to external piety: we have seen his love for building
and decorating churches, his contributions to the monastery, etc. His zeal for the memory of the holy founders
is particularly underscored. He found a miraculous icon
of the Mother of God, the *Odigitriia*, which had been
brought to the island by St. Savvatii. Filipp placed it
above St. Savvatii's grave. He put his stone cross in the
chapel where St. Herman lies. He corrected the old Psalter
which had belonged to St. Zosima and he liked to celebrate the liturgical services in his poor chasubles. He
requested that the lives of the Solovki saints be accompanied by a description of miracles, miracles which took
place after the saint's death and near the saint's grave.
Other things are precious for us. We hear that, from time
to time, the hegumen liked to seclude himself in a solitary
cell for prayer and contemplation. Filipp's hermitage,
two and one-half *versts* from the cloister, still reminds
us of the place of his solitude. Only prayer, of course,
could restore that spiritual life which was violated by
the constant burden of administrative and economic
concerns. Behind the mills and the salt works, we must
not overlook the humble wooden hermitage which saved
Filipp from the power of vanity, preserved the image of
the monk within the administrator, and which educated
him for the final feat of matyrdom.

Besides that, his very service as hegumen and the
uplifting of the economy in ways unfamiliar to him
prepared the martyr's crown for the saint. The hegumen
of the great northern monastery could not remain unknown to the Tsar.

We have already encountered Ivan Vasil'evich's
large land grants to the monastery. Some of these land
grants were not free of charge: some were rewards for
the right of tax-free trade in salt, a right taken away from
the monastery. Some were connected with the monastery's

obligation of cultivating neglected and unworked land. Still, the Tsar's special generosity to the distant monastery cannot be denied. Aside from the grants of land, we also have evidence of the Tsar's personal contributions to the monastery. The Tsar made a particularly large contribution (1,000 rubles) for the building of the Cathedral of the Transfiguration. The hegumen himself repeatedly asked the Tsar's help for his wide-spread building projects. The Tsar's gifts to the monastic vestry in the form of utensils, vessels, and crosses are known. Until the early part of the twentieth century, three altar crosses given by Ivan the Terrible were preserved in the monastery. All were of gold, decorated with rubies, pearls, and other stones. One is almost three pounds in weight. Signatures on them indicate the time and the title of the donor. Two of them date to Filipp's time. Among the Tsar's gifts, our attention is also drawn to a rare book — the translation of Flavius Josephus' *The Wars of the Jews*, which is indicative not so much of the scholarly interests of the Solovetskii hegumen as it is of the "humanistic" tastes of Ivan the Terrible.

If Ivan the Terrible did remember Fedor Kolychov from youth, the Tsar had occasion to see and evaluate the Solovetskii hegumen in Moscow itself. Evidence has been preserved that the Solovetskii hegumen was in Moscow at the Councils of 1550 and 1551. From these trips, Filipp brought the following gifts of the Tsar to Solovki: two satin, light-blue shrouds for coverings on the saints' coffins and two sacerdotal robes of white cloth studded with pearls.

For Filipp himself, his stay in Moscow during these years could not pass unnoticed. After a thirteen year absence, he again immersed himself in the sphere of Moscow social activities. *Rus'*, in one of its history's tensest moments, again rose behind the Solovetskii Mon-

astery. Moscow, it seemed, was experiencing an era of
complete renewal. Preparing for the victorious conquest
of Kazan', on the eve of unprecedented expansion of
Russian power in the East, Tsar Ivan Vasil'evich, in union
with the "chosen council" ["*izbrannaia rada*"] which was
led by Sil'vestr and Adashev, was feverishly carrying
through land reform. The revocation of local administration [*kormlenie*], the broad, self-government of the
regional territories [*volosti*], the revision of the Code of
Law [*Sudebnik*], and the reform of finances and the
military-landservice system followed one after the other.
This strenuous work of reform was imbued with a lofty
moral inspiration. The Tsar "together with his boyars
humbly asked for the forgiveness of his sins." Having
himself repented, he demanded repentance from the
whole land and a reconciliation of old injuries — especially
those caused by the boyars during his younger years.
And, finally, the Tsar thought of, and carried out, a com-
prehensive Church reform at the *Stoglav Sobor*. Problems
of Church administration and ritual, and various attitudes
within Church life, especially the monastic, were put
before the Council in question form by the Tsar. The
Tsar presented the new *Sudebnik* and the administrative
charters for regional self-government to the *Stoglav Sobor*
for its evaluation. Ivan did not yet distinguish between
lay and spiritual authority, between the sphere of the
Tsar and that of the clerics. "Reason out and confirm
according to the rules of the holy apostles and according
to the former laws of our ancestors so that all customs in
our Tsardom might be according to God." The Church
was summoned to bless the act of national renewal.

The hegumen of Solovki certainly participated in
the work of the *Stoglav Sobor* of 1551 along with other
monastic heads — "spiritual fathers" — and even anchorites
who were asked by the Tsar to attend. Filipp left Moscow

undoubtedly enriched by political, ecclesiastical, and social experience since he passed through a brief, but serious course of clerical leadership. The future appeared cloudless to contemporaries of this great epoch. Nothing adumbrated the coming storm.

No matter how far from Moscow the Solovetskii Monastery was "on the icy sea, in the land of the Karelian tongue, in the wild Lapland" (Kurbskii's words), it was, nevertheless, as we have already seen, in constant touch with the capital. Though with some delay, news of affairs in Moscow had to reach here. News reached the monastery by means of pilgrims, monks, monastic traders, and finally, by those in disfavor who were to be incarcerated in the monastery by order of the Tsar or the Council. We know of two of those who were exiled in Solovki during Filipp's rule: Artemii, hegumen of Holy Trinity Monastery and Sil'vestr, the well-known priest.

Hegumen Artemii was connected with the affair of the heresies of Matfei Bashkin and, together with the latter's disciples, was condemned at the Council of 1554. This was one of the last waves of that religious rationalism in *Rus'* at the end of the fifteenth century, a wave raised by the heresy of the Judaizers. Actually, Artemii was not convicted of heresy. He was able to refute the evidence of many "witnesses." He was blamed only for breaking fasts and for critical opinions which offended the ear of the pious. "Artemii spoke of the Trinity; in the book by Iosif of Volotsk it is written that God sent two angels to Sodom, that is to say, the Son and the Holy Spirit; and Artemii does not condemn the Novgorod heretics, praises the Latins, and does not keep the fast; he ate fish throughout Great Lent; on the day of the Holy Cross he ate fish at the table of the Grand Prince," etc. . . . For all these sins Artemii was defrocked and exiled to Solovki to be under the surveillance of "the spiritual head, hegumen Filipp." He was ordered to be kept in strict confinement, "in a quiet cell," and not to communicate with anyone other than the spiritual father and the hegumen, who was to "punish him and teach him Holy Scripture." Everything was to be reported to Archbishop Pimen of Novgorod, who was then to notify Moscow. The detailed document of the Council, which was sent to the Solovetskii hegumen and which contained the sentence with all its reasons and with the evidence of all the witnesses, has been preserved.

We do not know how St. Filipp treated the exiled hegumen. Among the hierarchs at the Council there was one (Kassian of Riazan') who took the side of the accused. Among the "heretics" condemned and exiled by the Council was Feodorit, the "enlightener" of the Laplanders, a monk from the Solovetskii Monastery who was soon forgiven. One of the Solovetskii elders, Asaf Belobaev, testified in favor of Artemii.

Be it as it may, the guarding of the Solovetskii prisoner was not too strict. Soon he was able to escape. Having made his way to Lithuania, he appears later in the sources as the defender of Orthodoxy, particularly against Feodosii Kosoi, similarly a Moscow fugitive who was condemned in connection with the same Bashkin case. This at least proves that Artemii's heresies were exaggerated in Moscow.

Some six years after Artemii's condemnation, one of his accusers had to share his fate — imprisonment in the Solovetskii Monastery. This was the famous priest, Sil'vestr, of whom the *Tsarstvennaia Kniga* (an official chronicle) wrote, reflecting the Tsar's irritation with the former favorite: "he ruled over everything by means of both ecclesiastical and governmental power, just like the Tsar and the Bishops; all he lacked was the throne and the name of Tsar; the ecclesiastical power, however, he already possessed." Hegumen Filipp certainly knew him well when in Moscow and saw him as the true inspirer of the government during the years of great reforms. His exile signified the collapse of such a triumphantly marked union of Tsar, Church, and People. The break in relations between the Tsar and his favorites, Sil'vestr and Adashev and their "selected council," had occurred earlier. Soon after the conquest of Kazan', the Tsar, during his serious illness, was sorrowfully convinced that his favorites supported Prince Vladimir Andreevich and not his son. He feared a repetition of boyar troubles. Sil'vestr had disagreements with the Tsarina and with her kin, the Romanovs, all of which aided the break. The Tsar felt the moral tutelage of the strict archpriest to be an ever-increasing burden. It seemed to him that the "chosen council" (the "gathering of dogs" ["*sobatskoe sobranie*"]) was taking all power from him. With a lack of character typical of weak natures, he long endured being surrounded by persons who were opposed to him. A basic difference of views about the Livonian War of 1558 made co-operation impossible. The Tsar was tormented by strange suspicions: the boyars, together with Sil'vestr, had — he thought — brought about the death of his wife, "separating him from his dove." Many fell from favor and executions began. Adashev's death saved him from the executioners. Sil'vestr was evidently tried at the Council where he was charged with poisoning the Tsarina. The very mildness of the punishment — exile to the monastery — reveals that nobody believed these accusations.

St. Filipp realized that Sil'vestr, as no one else in Solovki, could inform him of Muscovite events. We can surmise that they hardly differed in their evaluation of the situation. They both obviously lamented the Tsar's moral fall — the depravity, the disgraceful behavior, and the executions which took on the nature of bloody orgies. In the years preceding the establishment of the *oprichnina*, 1560-1564, executions were infrequent. But the impression on contemporaries was strong. The victims were sometimes worthy people (Prince Repnin) or completely innocent ones (Adashev's relatives).

From the time of the establishment of the *oprichnina* (January, 1565), executions take on a mass character. Stories circulated about many of those killed, stories which pictured them as martyrs, almost saints. It was said that Dmitrii Shevyrev, when impaled, "sang from memory the canon to our Lord Jesus Christ and also the *akathist* hymn to the Blessed Mother of God." Before his execution, the young Gorbachev took the already chopped off head of his father into his hands and prayed, thanking God "that he had considered them to be worthy of being killed while innocent."

The attitude of the Solovetskii hegumen to the new, terrible institute was totally unwavering. Soon he would publicly defend his belief in Moscow. In the spring of 1566, when Metropolitan Afanasii left his chair, St. Filipp received the Tsar's letter inviting him to come to Moscow "for spiritual counsel." Did he guess that the Tsar had selected him to succeed the departed hierarch? The Tsar's letter could have been a simple invitation to the *Zemskii Sobor* which, as we know, was being convened in the summer of 1566. We will return to this question in the next chapter.

The hegumen departed from the tearful brethren. However, not everyone's tears were sincere. Some parted from the holy hegumen without regret. Again Filipp went to Moscow through Novgorod by the same route he had taken when he originally came to Solovki. Perhaps he wanted to meet with Archbishop Pimen, but he did not find him in the diocese. Pimen was already in Moscow.

It is said that the citizens of Novgorod came out to meet Filipp three *versts* from the city with bread and salt, begging him to petition the Tsar for "their fatherland," Great Novgorod, whom the Tsar's wrath was already hanging. Perhaps the *Life* here anticipates both the lofty destiny of Filipp and the tragic lot of the city, a city native to him through the blood of his ancestors.

Listening to the suffering of the people and preparing to speak courageously on behalf of the people before the Tsar, Filipp went to Moscow where the white cowl and the martyr's crown awaited him.

CHAPTER THREE

ST. FILIPP—METROPOLITAN

What were the relations now being formed between the Tsar and the Metropolitan, whose chair was destined to be occupied by Filipp? We left the affairs of the Moscow Metropolitanate when young Fedor Kolychov had left Moscow. At that time the office was occupied by Metropolitan Daniil, a scholarly but obsequious hierarch who was under the control of the Grand Prince. In Ivan the Terrible's youth, the boyar parties displayed even less respect for Church authorities than the sovereigns did. Daniil was deposed by Shuiskii in 1539 and exiled to the Volokolamsk Monastery where he had previously been hegumen. Later he was forced to sign a document in which he renounced his chair "after having more reasonably scrutinized both my infirmity for such a task and my sinful thoughts" — an abasement from which even the notorious heretic Zosima had been spared when deposed from the metropolitanate "because of illness." The same fate befell Daniil's successor, Ioasaf, chosen from the hegumens of Holy Trinity Monastery. Metropolitan Makarii, an historian of the Russian Church, observes the following about his selection by the council: "The Churchmen sinned much since they, probably yielding to pressure from worldly power, elected and confirmed the new metropolitan before the then metropolitan had renounced his chair." Placed in the metro-

politanate by the Shuiskiis, Ioasaf drew their ire by going
over to the side of the Belskiis. During the consequent
overthrow organized by the Shuiskiis, the metropolitan
was subjected to severe humiliation and coercion. The
conspirators surrounded his cell and threw rocks at it.
They pursued him in the Court, ripped off his mantle,
and almost killed him. The deposed metropolitan died
in Holy Trinity Monastery.

In the sad history of Church-State relations in the
sixteenth century, Metropolitan Makarii's time (1542-
1564) is a period of fortunate reaction. Spiritual authority
had not been so elevated for a long time. Though obligated to the Shuiskii revolt for his election, and having
experienced quite a few offenses from boyar self-rule in
the first few years, Makarii managed to hold on. He was
unbending when encountering the powerful and he acted
as a peacemaker in courtly disputes. Interceding before
the boyars on behalf of persons who had the misfortune
of arousing their hatred (Vorontsov), he pleaded before
the sovereign, who had already thrown off boyar trustee-
ship replacing those boyars with impartial boyars who
had been in disfavor. Makarii's influence on the young
Tsar was great and beneficial. The metropolitan was the
most learned scholar of his time, having worked for
many years on his colossal work, the *Chetii-minei*, in
which he intended to collect "all the books which were
read in the Russian land." Undoubtedly Ivan the Terrible's
brilliant education and his broad historical ideas were
the result of his close association with Makarii. He had
no other teachers. Makarii's moral and social influence
was later reenforced by the incomparably more energetic
and powerful influence of Sil'vestr. It is noteworthy that
Sil'vestr was one of Makarii's collaborators in Novgorod
and came to Moscow with him. In their persons, as later
in the person of St. Filipp, the cultural and free influence

of Novgorod worked beneficiently on a demoralized
Moscow. But Metropolitan Makarii, in contrast to the
"chosen council," was not a politician but a man of
scholarly, private work. He did not impose his views
on the Tsar and thereby was able to preserve his moral
authority after the fall of the council. His intercession
on behalf of the disgraced Sil'vestr was unsuccessful,
but to the end of Makarii's life, the Tsar maintained
his respect for this hierarch. There were cases where
he accepted his solicitations and rendered mercy to his
real or imagined enemies "for his father, Metropolitan
Makarii." In 1556 Ivan wrote to Gurii, the Archbishop
of Kazan' : "O God, how happy the Russian land would
be if the hierarchs were like the Right Reverend Makarii
and you." However, with the years, this noble role of
petitioner before the Tsar who had lost his moral balance
became increasingly more difficult. Impatient people
like Prince Kurbskii reproached the Metropolitan for
weakness. Makarii often thought of leaving, as he reveals
in his own spiritual testament. But he remained, bowing
before the requests of the Tsar and the Church. Finally,
death freed Makarii from his difficult position on December 31, 1563.

Afanasii, a monk of the Chudov Monastery and
the Tsar's spiritual father, was chosen as his successor.
Before the election the Tsar wanted to adorn the chair
of the Metropolitanate of Moscow. The Council of
February 1564, however, had determined that future
metropolitans wear a white cowl (rather than the black)
"with chasubles and with the cherubim sewn on each
shoulder" and that they write documents in red according
to the example of the Archbishop of Novgorod. These
external distinctions were a poor substitute for that
decline in spiritual authority which marked the short
(two years) rule of Afanasii. Upset by Kurbskii's betrayal

and planning an unprecedented reprisal against the boyars, the Tsar wished to throw off — decisively and as a matter of principle — the Church's religious and moral check on himself, especially the restraint exercised on him by the person of the metropolitan. That was the meaning of the tragi-comedy of the Tsar's departure to the Aleksandrovskii settlement [*sloboda*] which preceded the establishment of the *oprichnina*. In the message that the Tsar sent to Moscow from the settlement, a message which contained an explanation of the reasons for his anger at the whole "land," the clergy stood in the forefront: "The Tsar and Grand Prince is angered at the clergy which prays for him; at the archbishops, the bishops, the archimandrites, and the hegumens; and at his boyars, the *d'iaki*, the lesser gentry, and all administrative people." Having characterized the wilfulness and the selfishness of the boyars, the Tsar continues: "And the Tsar wished in whatever matters to begin to investigate and punish his boyars, all administrative people, and also the serving princes and the lesser gentry. And the archbishops, the bishops, the archimandrites, and the hegumens, together with the boyars and the courtiers, the *d'iaki*, and all the administrative people began to cover up before the sovereign and Grand Prince." In view of all this, the Tsar announced that he "had left his government and had gone to dwell where his sovereign, the Lord, may teach him."

The Church was the only power that could limit the Tsar's tyranny. Ivan the Terrible could expect no opposition to his bloody measures from the ruling class and certainly none from the masses. The Tsar's right to "remove anyone from favor" ["*opala*"] or to execute was recognized by all. Only the Church, if not disputing the right, either pointed out the Tsar's duty or called for mercy, a mercy which was above the law. It was precisely to throw off this last and bothersome leash that Ivan performed the comedy of renouncing the throne. All this resulted in a formal affirmation of his unlimited right of execution.

The bishops, with Pimen of Novgorod at their head (the metropolitan had remained in Moscow to look after its spiritual affairs), and the boyars, in the name of all the people, begged the sovereign to return and rule according to his total will. For the Church, this was a renunciation of her ancient right of intercession [*pechalovanie*]. Nevertheless, in the following years we have two notes signed by Metropolitan Afanasii and other bishops and boyars. These notes supported two magnates, Ivan Petrovich Iakovlev and Prince Mikhail Ivanovich Vorotynskii, both "disfavored" by the Tsar. The Tsar now reconsidered, "forgiving the guilt" of his servants who had committed an offense "because of the request of his father, Afanasii" (1565-1566). This indicates that Afanasii too did not remain totally indifferent to the violence of the *oprichnina*. But his good will was already broken by the capitulation at the Aleksandrovskii settlement. The Tsar's return to Moscow was marked by unprecedented and refined executions. The Church kept silent. Within a year, the metropolitan's strength ebbed. He left the metropolitanate on May 19, 1566 "because of great infirmity" in order to return to his Chudov Monastery. That was when the Tsar summoned Filipp.

Actually, he made perhaps one more experiment. At least Kurbskii reports that prior to summoning Filipp, the Tsar had turned to Herman, Archbishop of Kazan', who was later canonized, and begged him to accept the election to the metropolitanate. Kurbskii even asserted that Herman was "forced to do this by the council," i.e. that his election had already occurred in the council. The designated metropolitan had already, "as it is related," been living at the metropolitanate's quarters for two days. He was still undecided about accepting the heavy burden when he and the Tsar had a disagreement precisely on the question of the *oprichnina*. In a private conversation with the Tsar, the cleric, in "quiet and humble words," reminded the Tsar of God's frightful judgment, imposed on all, "on Tsars and on simple people." The Tsar returned to his "favored ones," told them of this conversation, and met with general indignation from them: "God save you from such advice. Do you, Tsar, wish to be again in an even more pitiful bondage to that bishop than you were for so many years to Aleksei and Sil'vestr?" Aleksei Basmanov and his son even hugged his knees, begging the Tsar not to yield to the bishop's suggestions. The hint that Sil'vestr's guardianship had been a burden to the Tsar's self-esteem produced an immediate effect. The Tsar ordered Herman to be sent away from the Church chambers with the words: "You have not yet been elevated to the metropolitanate and yet you are already trying to bind me." Kurbskii ends his story with a report that the Archbishop of Kazan' was found dead in his court two days later — some say from poison, others from suffocation. Here Kurbskii clearly errs. Archbishop Herman participated in the enthronement of Metropolitan Filipp on July 25 and died on November 6, 1567. This error casts a shadow over Kurbskii's report. All Russian historians, however, have accepted the actual fact of Herman's election. Even the conversation between the "favored ones" and Ivan the Terrible are psychologically quite accurate. Even if they are contrived, they illustrate excellently the Tsar's weak spot upon which the *oprichniki* play. Ivan the Terrible's correspondence with Kurbskii speaks of his unusual sensitivity to attempts to "bind" him morally. Finally, the election of Filipp produced analogous scenes, even preserved in an official act.

In the summer of that very year, 1566, a *Zemskii Sobor* convened in Moscow to consider the problem of continuing the Livonian War in the light of the conditions proposed by the Polish King for a truce. In the verdict, given on July 2, there are, first of all, the names of many clerical figures — nine bishops, many hegumens, and even simple monks. Pimen of Novgorod and Herman of Kazan' signed first. Among the hegumens of distant monasteries, those of Novgorod and Pskov, we do not find the signature of the Solovetskii hegumen. At this time he was certainly on the way to Moscow. The clergy participating in the *Zemskii Sobor*, meeting and voting separately, could constitute an authentic Church council for the election of the metropolitan. It was precisely at this time, before or after the political conference, that the council could have chosen Herman. Considering the factor of time, we are led to conclude that Filipp received his invitation to Moscow even before his candidacy for the chair of the metropolitanate had been advanced. Having arrived late for the political conference, he arrived precisely when the Tsar, after his quarrel with Herman, had excluded the latter from candidacy. This is the most probable interpretation of events if we do not wish to discard completely Kurbskii's report.

In accepting this sequence of events, we face yet another difficulty, this time a psychological one. What forced Ivan the Terrible to turn specifically to Filipp after his failure with Herman? In the person of Herman, a holy man had been called to the metropolitanate. The demands stated by this saint turned out to be unacceptable to the Tsar. Did the Tsar really think that Filipp would be more acquiescent? And how could he err so seriously in his new choice?

We feel it would be unfair to Ivan the Terrible's complex character if we were to explain his actions solely by base motives. A contradiction of inner motives is unusually characteristic for a Tsar who always combined his evil deeds with a passionate piety. Ivan the Terrible undoubtedly displayed a zeal for the purity and grandeur of the Church — external and internal. His accusations against contemporary monks, accusations replete with unkind irony, were dictated by that very zeal. He wanted to see a holy pastor in the Cathedral of the Assumption of the Mother of God. There is little doubt about that. But it is just as doubtless that he wanted to retain complete freedom of action for himself. He wanted to have a truly devout saint but not a judge of his conscience. That is why, after his experience with Herman, he does not turn to Pimen or to one of the more complaisant hierarchs, but rather seeks the most worthy one — and he finds whom he sought in the person of the hegumen of the Solovetskii Monastery, a person long known to him.

Under Ivan the Terrible the election of metropolitans took place at councils, i.e. they were externally canonical even though they were wholly determined by the Tsar's will. The Tsar's will appears at the forefront of an unusual official act compiled at Filipp's election. Because of the document's extraordinary significance, we quote it in full:

In the summer of 7074 [1566], on July 20, Tsar and Grand Prince Ivan Vasil'evich of all Russia, together with the archbishops, bishops, and the archimandrites, and with the whole devout council of the Transfiguration of Jesus Christ our God and the great Solovetskii miracle-workers Zosima and Savvatii, compelled hegumen Filipp to the metropolitanate.

And hegumen Filipp said that the Tsar and Grand
Prince should leave aside the *oprichnina*. And should
the Tsar and Grand Prince not abandon the *oprichnina*,
it would be impossible for him to be metropolitan.
And even though he be selected for the metropolitanate, he would still have to leave the post thereafter. The Tsar should concentrate on bringing unity
to the land as before. And the Tsar and Grand Prince
spoke with the archbishops and bishops about this.
The archbishops and bishops petitioned the Tsar and
Grand Prince about his royal anger. And the Tsar and
Grand Prince set aside his anger and told hegumen
Filipp to speak to the archbishops and bishops, that
hegumen Filipp postpone such questions, that he not
interfere with the *oprichnina* and with the Tsar's
daily affairs but rather be placed upon the metropolitanate. Upon Filipp's accession, the Tsar and
Grand Prince would not revoke the *oprichnina*; and
Filipp was commanded not to interfere in the Tsar's
daily affairs. He should not leave the metropolitanate
and should consult with the Tsar and Grand Prince
just as former metropolitans consulted with the
Tsar's father, Grand Prince Ivan. And hegumen Filipp,
at the request of the Tsar, gave his word to the archbishops and bishops that he, by the word of the Tsar
and by their blessing, accepts the metropolitanate
freely, that he would not interfere with the *oprichnina* and with the Tsar's daily affairs, and that upon
accession he would not leave the metropolitanate
because of the *oprichnina* or the Tsar's daily affairs.
And to confirm this verdict, the archbishops and
bishops, and Filipp, the hegumen from Solovki just
named to the metropolitanate, have affixed their
signatures. [Signatures follow].

From this official entry it is observed that the

election of Filipp was accompanied by stormy scenes. The "Tsar's anger" was provoked because Filipp stipulated his agreement with a definite demand — the revocation of the *oprichnina*. The Solovetskii hegumen's motivation shows splendidly how well-versed he was in the events of contemporary Russian life. "And even though he be selected for the metropolitanate, he would still have to leave the post thereafter." The experience of the last two or three metropolitans is contained in these words. With the existence of the *oprichnina* there cannot be normal relations between the ruling spheres of hierarch and Tsar. The metropolitan could not carry out clerical social service. The Tsar did not accept this condition but he made a concession which is hidden in the authoritative form of "command." He allowed Filipp to "advise" just as previous metropolitans "had consulted with his father and grandfather." With this the right of intercession [*pechalovanie*], done away with in 1565 with the introduction of the *oprichnina*, was re-established. With such a stipulation, St. Filipp allowed the hierarchs to convince him. He accepted the election and gave his word "not to interfere with the *oprichnina*." The very composition of the protocol which has come down to us, ratified by the members of the council and the designated metropolitan, had, of course, the goal of securing the metropolitan's obligation before the Tsar. By this act Ivan sought to secure himself against any possible future incursions by the hierarch into that sphere which he viewed as his own "daily concern." One might think that great pressure was put on Filipp by the hierarchs and that he yielded to it. However, it is impossible to ignore the fact that among the signatures of the hierarchs the names of two are missing. These two were apparently in Moscow at the time because at the beginning of July they signed the decision of the *Zemskii Sobor* and five

days after Filipp's election they participated in his triumphant consecration. These missing signatures belong
to Herman of Kazan' and Elevferii of Suzdal'. The name
of St. Herman, who had just courageously accused the
Tsar, leads to the conjecture that not all bishops were
inclined to bless this capitulation to the Tsar by the newly
elected metropolitan. For them, as for Filipp, the *oprichnina* probably constituted too serious an obstacle to peace
both in society and in the Church.

Filipp's compliance can, of course, be explained
by the influence of the majority of hierarchs in which
the humble Solovetskii hegumen apparently saw the'
"voice" of the Russian Church. It can also be explained
by the Tsar's pliability. Filipp refused to fight the *oprichnina* as an institution but he did not refuse to struggle
against its excesses. The return to the Church of its right
to intercede [*pechalovanie*] gave him some hope of
alleviating the horrors of the *oprichnina*. His electoral
capitulation can certainly be interpreted in this way.

But in so interpreting it and in treating with reverence the purity which inspired his intentions, we cannot
but see in the hesitations and concession a certain weakness shown by the hierarch at the threshold of his new
service. The July days of his life remind us remarkably
well of his first days as hegumen on Solovki. These valuable tiny traits which so palely fill in his portrait speak of
the same thing: in Filipp's nature there was no energetic
authoritativeness, no total confidence in himself, or no
firm knowledge of his goals and means. His first inclination
is to run from the heavy burden. But, once having accepted it, he bears it faithfully and courageously. His
powers grow under the weight of the burden. New, un-
suspected aspects of his personality appear. Filipp, the
"master" of the Solovetskii monastery, seems a completely different person from Filipp the "sufferer" for

the whole Russian land. Yet he is still the same. The power of God was accomplished in his weakness and grace compensated for his natural lack.

On July 24, four days after the signing of the electoral document, the official election of Filipp took place in the presence of the Tsar and the whole blessed council. "And he was then elevated to the metropolitan's court." And on yet another day, on July 25, the triumphant consecration of the new metropolitan took place in the Cathedral of the Assumption. We possess the ceremony of this consecration as it was performed in Moscow in the sixteenth century. Let us borrow the details from Metropolitan Makarii's description:

> On the day designated for the consecration of the metropolitan, a special elevation was built in front of the ambo of the Cathedral of the Assumption. Two chairs were placed upon it, one on the right side for the Tsar, the other on the left for the Archbishop [of Novgorod, the oldest in the Russian Church. G. F.]. A bit lower, on both sides, long benches were placed for the bishops. On the floor in front of the elevation, a large eagle was drawn with spread wings. Before the liturgy, the designated one was led from the altar in his full vestments and placed standing on the eagle. Upon completion of the Thrice-Holy Hymn, he was invested as bishop-metropolitan and he then continued and completed the liturgy himself. . .
> Upon completion of the liturgy, the bishops took the new primate by the arms, led him to the elevation in the middle of the church and there thrice seated him pronouncing "eis polla eti, Despota." After this, the metropolitan took off his vestments. The hierarchs then placed the Panagia, a mantle

with *istochniki*, placed a white cowl on him, and
then led him to the metropolitan's place. The
sovereign then approached the metropolitan and
presented him with the primate's staff [once belonging to St. Peter of Moscow — G. F.] and spoke
the following words: "The All-Powerful and Life-
Giving Holy Trinity which has given us autocracy
over the Russian realm of all Rus' grants you this
great throne of the great miracle-worker Peter's
hierarchy, the metropolitanate of all Russia and
of the Russian realm by means of investment by
the holy fathers, the archbishops, and the bishops
of our autocratic Russian realm. Accept the staff
of ecclesiastical rule, ascend to the ancient seat,
and pray to God and all the saints for us and our
children and for all Orthodox, and for the good
of all Orthodox Christianity, both physically and
spiritually. And may the Lord grant you health
and long life forever and ever, amen." The metropolitan answered the sovereign with these words:
"May the all-mighty and all-powerful hand of the
Most High Lord God preserve your Russian kingdom and you, autocratic Tsar and lord. May your
kingdom be in peace and endure for many years,
and may it be victorious over all those obedient
to you forever and ever . . . Health, health, health!
Long live the life-bearing sovereign and autocrat,
the doer of good."

Upon leaving the cathedral, the metropolitan,
dressed in the mantle, accepted the holy cross of
the Life-Giving Tree, sat upon the donkey which
had been readied and rode to the court of the
Grand Prince to bless him. The metropolitan's
donkey was led by the Grand Prince's equerry and

by the metropolitan's boyar. Two choirs, one representing the State and the other the metropolitanate, went before them singing verses. Four priests carrying palms walked in front of the singers. After blessing the sovereign in his court, the metropolitan then rode to his own court where he blessed the hierarchs and the clergy, then rode around the Kremlin blessing the people and the city. He then went again to the sovereign and returned finally to his own chambers where a meal was offered to all the participants of the celebration. Sometimes the meal was offered by the sovereign in his own chambers.

Such a celebration took place in Moscow on July 25, 1566 with nine hierarchs participating. This time neither Herman nor Elevferii declined to participate. Pimen was first in attendance. St. Filipp was destined to accept the stole [*omofor*] from the hands of the bishop who became his betrayer and the crozier from the hands of the Tsar who killed him. The *Life* has Filipp delivering a didactic speech to the Tsar on this day. Since it does not carry the stamp of authenticity, we will analyze it later, together with others in which it may be possible to extract at least a reflection of his views.

The celebrations ended and the difficulties of St. Filipp's new service began. It seemed that the dark forebodings which held sway over him during the election were dissipating. It pleased providence to postpone his confessional sacrifice for a time. The horrors of the *oprichnina* ceased and over the course of a year and a half we do not hear of executions in Moscow. The destructive establishment continued to function, of course, poisoning and corrupting the whole national body. But at the top, in direct proximity to the Tsar, there was a respite from the flow of blood. Undoubtedly the courageous acts, one after the other, of two saints could not pass without leaving a trace on the Tsar's impressionable soul. There was also another reason for his restraint. At the *Zemskii Sobor* all classes had just expressed the same understanding of national interests, an equal readiness to bear sacrifices for the State. The Livonian War was one of Ivan the Terrible's most bloody affairs. Because of this war he quarreled with the "Chosen Council" once and for all. Unity with the people on this question, or with the ruling circles of the people, had to calm the Tsar's suspicions and soften his lack of trust in the *zemshchina*. First in the Moscow delegation which took the Tsar's unacceptable demands to Sigismund Augustus was boyar Fedor Ivanovich Umnyi-Kolychov, the metropolitan's cousin. His appointment occurred a few days before Filipp's accession.

Very little information about the administrative activity of St. Filipp as Metropolitan of Moscow has been preserved. Filipp's *Life*, in giving a general evaluation of this side of Filipp's activity, notes that he attempted in everything to imitate Metropolitan Makarii, his worthy predecessor. From everything which is known about Filipp's administrative activity, it can be safely said that St. Filipp took upon himself not only the burden of rule in the Moscow eparchy but also burdened himself with the care of the entire Russian Church. A metropolitan in the fifteenth and sixteenth century corresponded to the patriarch of the seventeenth century. He had to appoint bishops to all the eparchies, watch over their activity, admonish and correct them by means of messages, and call them to Moscow in case of necessity. He could not however try bishops, a right which belonged only to a council. But the responsibility of convening councils lay with the metropolitan and in the sixteenth century councils were convened quite frequently — as a rule, once a year, sometimes more.

At the beginning of the sixteenth century the metropolitan's patrimonies were still scattered over fifteen districts. In seven of these districts there were 531 villages and settlements and 1,818 peasants. By the middle of the sixteenth century these holdings increased greatly. At the end of the century their income, according to Possevino, was about 22,000 thalers and, according to Fletcher, about 3,000 rubles (equivalent to about 180,000 to 210,000 rubles in the nineteenth century). However, the holdings and incomes of the Archbishop of Novgorod far exceeded those of the Metropolitan of Moscow.

If the administration of Church properties demanded managerial attention, then so also did the metropolitan's court. The sphere of its jurisdiction encompassed both clerical and lay affairs. As any bishop, the metropolitan had his boyars, his secretaries [d'iaki], his courtiers and his officials [desiatinniki] — in short the metropolitan had an entire administrative apparatus built on the model of an appanage principality.

Some fragmentary evidence has come down to us concerning certain daily acts in Metropolitan Filipp's administrative work. We see him consecrating the bishops of Polotsk and of Rostov and consecrating churches. The first months of Filipp's rule were darkened by a horrible national disaster — the plague. The epidemic approached the Moscow districts; it was carried to Moscow by the army which had been stationed on the Western border which was enveloped by war. People died in great numbers from "the evil infection." The metropolitan's intervention was necessitated — priestless parishes needed replacements: ". . . priests had died and there was even no one to bury the dead." On September first the disease appeared in Mozhaisk, threatening Moscow itself. The Tsar set up a quarantine "of guard and post" in the zone of the plague;

he ordered no one to go from it to Moscow or back. In
the spring of 1567 the plague stopped for a time. Moscow
was able to be saved mainly because of the government's
energetic measures.

One of the rare records of Metropolitan Filipp's
economic-administrative concerns is Prince Vladimir
Andreevich Staritskii's charter granting properties [*zhalovannaia gramota*] which was issued in the metropolitan's
name. This charter stipulated that all the metropolitan's
villages and monasteries which were within the Prince's
appanage were freed from taxes and payments to the
appanage household and were freed from the appanage
court "except for murder or for red-handed thievery."
"And our father, Metropolitan Filipp of all Russia, or
his boyars, will judge these cases." It is perhaps possible
to detect in this act the vestige of the friendship between
the Staritskii princes and the Kolychovs. Filipp's father
had been Prince Andrei's loyal servant. Andrei's son,
dragging out his life under the threat of the Tsar's suspicions and having taken his brother to a monastery on
the eve of his own death, expressed his gratitude in this
charter to the metropolitan for the loyal service of Filipp's
father.

Although the records of Metropolitan Filipp's
administrative activity are quite scant, we do have evidence
indicating that Filipp did not forget the distant, northern
monastery which had cultivated his spiritual life. He obviously returned frequently in thought to the happy
working years in Solovki and he obviously turned in prayer
to the Solovetskii saints for help and intercession with the
anxieties of Moscow life. Within the metropolitan's house
he organized a chapel named after St. Zosima and St.
Savvatii. Many years later Patriarch Nikon, a successor
and admirer of Filipp, dedicated this very chapel to
Filipp the Apostle, St. Filipp's guardian angel.

Four letter-documents of Metropolitan Filipp have been preserved in the Solovetskii archive — three to Solovki and one to the Novgorod homesteaders of the monastery. These letters are full of managerial and economic concern and of instructions; these letters breathe forth the former hegumen's fatherly feeling for the monastery which he left behind.

In the first letter Filipp informs his brethren of his election to the chair of All Rus' and bids that they choose a hegumen according to their own will and that he will ask the Tsar to confirm their choice. In the second letter he lists the gifts which are being sent to the monastery. These are icons, crosses, money, and "spices" — pepper, saffron and ginger. Both letters are addressed to the brethren of whom elders Iona and Paisii are cited by name. The third letter, to Novgorod, is to the elder Isaak. It is devoted to the conditions of transferring to the monastery the property of a Novgorodian named Tuchka. There is a promise to request the Tsar "to rehabilitate that household and garden," i.e. to free it from taxes.

These three letters were sent in the first days of Filipp's post as primate. The fourth letter was written on January 30, 1568, precisely during the difficult time when the struggle with the Tsar was commencing. And its content is troublesome. Evidently the good relations between the metropolitan and Solovki became beclouded, for the monks had caused the hierarch in Moscow to become "very sorrowful." He reprimanded them for disobeying him; they had sent him "fish" for a funeral report . . . And the fish itself turned out to be "small and there was little of the medium-sized," i.e. the hierarch was shown a clear lack of consideration . . . The other matter which grieved the metropolitan was the fate of the works which were not completed while he was in Solovki. He hopes to convince Paisii and the brothers to clear the pond ("Holy Lake") which was dug while he was there. Not relying on the brethren to continue the work begun by him of their own free will, he promises to feed the laborers with his own bread: "and should you not grant this, should this not be done, you should so inform me." The entire letter is permeated with a bitterness which is not softened by the financial offer of giving the brethren their board. We do not know the reasons for the coolness toward the former hegumen and present metropolitan. Was it only for economic negligence that he deserved Filipp's reproach? Be that as it may, the hierarch's letter certainly had to sting him. He soon had occasion to pay back his spiritual father.

Besides these letters, the only other document of St. Filipp which has come down to us was addressed to the Kirillov-Belozersk Monastery and probably represents an example of the letters sent to all the most important monasteries in the fall of 1567 during the Tsar's campaign against Lithuania. In this document, however, it is no longer the former hegumen speaking but rather the head of the Russian Church in its inseparable link with Russian Orthodox Tsardom. The metropolitan asks the monks to pray for the Tsar, his family, and for the success of the Lithuanian campaign. "Because of our sins the godless Crimean Khan, Devlet-Girei — with all his Muhammedanism and Latinism — and the Lithuanian King, Sigismund Augustus and the heathen Germans who have fallen into many different heresies — primarily into Lutheranism — these forces have ravaged holy Christian churches and have desecrated holy and venerable icons . . . And hearing of these things, God's holy, anointed Tsar and Sovereign, Grand Prince Ivan Vasil'evich, autocrat of All Rus', was greatly insulted and saddened by what happened to the Church and to the holy, venerable icons . . . and with our blessing, and that of the whole blessed council, he and his forces went against his enemies on behalf of our holy churches, our holy, venerable icons, our holy, pious Christian faith which follows the Greek canons. He and his forces went against his enemies to protect his princely fatherland, to defend the Russian realm, entrusted to him by God, not only unto blood but even unto death."

The style of this letter of the metropolitan's corresponds fully to the official ideology of Ivan the Terrible's military endeavors. The Tsar liked to clothe his political acts — for example, the taking of Polotsk — in the form of a holy war against the enemies of faith and Church and in the name of triumphant Orthodoxy. The governmental chronicle has preserved for us clear evidence of these attitudes. But Ivan the Terrible's campaign, commencing so triumphantly in the autumn of 1567, became sluggish and ended in nothing. The Tsar, having personally participated in it, returned to the Aleksandrovskii settlement [*sloboda*] without victory and without glory. The moral help of the *zemshchina*, declared in July of 1566, brought no realistic results, results which the Tsar had counted on. He was now looking for something upon which to vent his irritation.

The terror of the *oprichnina* under Ivan the Terrible had its own rhythm of rise and fall. Karamzin calculated six "epochs of execution." Sometimes a connection can be established between the growing wave of terror and the failures of domestic policy. Kurbskii's flight and his devastating attack on the region of Great Lutsk [*Velikolutsk*] were a prelude to the establishment of the *oprichnina* itself — "the second epoch of executions" (1565). The unsuccessful campaign of 1567 precedes the new, increasingly fearful wave against which St. Filipp attempted to struggle and which subsided not long after his demise (1568-1571). This wave was the bloodiest of all. But before we move on to the events which brought about the tragic clash between the Metropolitan and Tsar, it is appropriate to sketch — in the most general terms — the character of the *oprichnina* in action, in its daily setting, and in its principles. As we shall see, St. Filipp's opposition was ultimately directed not only against the excesses of this institution but against the system itself. It is essential to consider whether St. Filipp, in his struggle against the *oprichnina*, is the spokesman of Christian conscience and the voice of the Russian people or, as many have thought, the spokesman of the "reactionary" aspirations of the defeated boyars.

CHAPTER FOUR

THE OPRICHNINA

The question of the *oprichnina* has become one of the major themes of historical scholarship. The generation of Russian scholars at the turn of the century examined the question again from a new point of view. Some new materials were used and it seems as though the riddle which tormented many from the sixteenth through seventeenth centuries has been satisfactorily solved.

We now know that this was not only a system of terror but a system of rule. From the very establishment of this institution in January 1565, Ivan the Terrible had demanded that the Muscovites grant him the right "to disfavor, to execute, to possess their lives and properties, and to establish the *oprichnina* in his government: there was to be established a special, private court for him and for all his household." This enormous task — the construction of the "Tsar's special, private household" — soon commenced. At first 1,000, then up to 6,000 of the state servitors [*sluzhilye liudi*] — those from the bottom of this class who were not connected by birth to princely or boyar leadership — were taken into the *oprichnina*. Districts in the central and northern part of the realm were set aside for their settlement. Former landowners were expelled to outlying districts. This partitioning and transferring of the state servitors [*sluzhilye liudi*] lasted many years and constituted a steady

99

social background for the bloody patterns of terror. In Moscow a series of "blocks" or parts of the city (on the Arbat and neighboring streets) were seized for the *oprichnina* and the former owners were simply expelled. The Tsar himself left the Kremlin and moved to a new *oprichnina* palace on the Arbat "by the Rizpolozhenskie Gates." Everything which was not a part of the *oprichnina* was officially called the *zemshchina*. "*Oprichnina*" Russia, just like the *zemshchina*, was headed by its own central institutions, its own government departments [*prikazy*], and it possessed its own treasury. The government, it turned out, was split into two parts. The old boyar *duma* with the same personnel — Prince Bel'skii and Prince Mstislavskii — remained at the head of the *zemshchina*. At the head of the *oprichnina* was the Tsar's court and the gentry of lower birth (Viazemskii was the only prince there). Dualism in government reached its acme when Ivan the Terrible placed the converted Tatar Khan, Simeon Bekbulatovich, at the head of the *zemshchina* (1575-1577) with the title "Grand Prince of All Rus'." For himself Ivan retained the humble title of the "Prince of Moscow." Of course this masquerade did not last long. But it reveals significantly the political idea at the root of the *oprichnina*.

It is clear that the political idea of the *oprichnina* was essentially the creation of a new administration and a new servitor class, one which was alien to the former traditions of the *zemshchina* and independent of boyar influence. The Tsar felt powerless to re-create the old order by means of reform or by changing the personnel of the ruling class. He built a new, parallel government organization in a new place and by using new people. The paradox of this revolution is that, although directed against the remains of the appanage tradition, it was itself vested in appanage forms. The very word "*oprichnina*" is taken from appanage life. In ancient times it signified the widow's share which the prince relegated to his widowed princess in his last will. Ivan the Terrible persistently, though hypocritically, emphasized the fiction that the *oprichnina* was only his "household," the organization of his court, that the old order was preserved in the government, in the *zemshchina*. "Ivashka," the appanage Prince of Moscow, wrote humble petitions to "the Grand Prince of All Rus' " asking him "to grant him permission . . . to move people. . ."

The psychology of weakness is hidden behind this dismal buffoonery: a weakness before the forces of tradition, before the age-old structure behind which stood the moral powers of national consciousness and the Church. In Ivan the Terrible's will of 1572 this sense of powerlessness takes on a maniacal aspect. The Tsar pictures himself as "exiled by the boyars and as wandering about the nations." His sons seemingly will have to "moderate their government." In short, Ivan the Terrible lives, if not in reality then at least psychologically, in the atmosphere of civil war.

The social make-up of the *oprichnina* also corresponded to its political goal. The dislocation of large masses of the servitor class [*sluzhilye liudi*] from the center to the outlying districts and even beyond certainly caused a break in the agricultural and moral ties of the people, a break between the peasants and the descendants of the "little appanage princes." In former times the Moscow government, in annexing appanages and free Russian lands, "took" many hundreds of the best people to Moscow, thus destroying the aristocratic leadership of the local society. This system of "taking people to Moscow" [*vyvod na Moskvu*] was applied by Ivan the Terrible to almost the whole composition of the servitor class — not only to "small princes" and boyars but to whole districts of central Moscow. This was a social upheaval which encompassed all levels of Russian society, even the very bottom of the social structure.

Contemporaries testify that the operation of "taking people to Moscow" was accompanied by administrative cruelties which tended to give it the character of a national calamity. Landowners chased from their former property "were not allowed to take any of their moveable property." They were simply "driven out with their wives and children, placed on the main road, and were sometimes forced to make their way by foot to their new places and to feed off handouts." The ruination of the landowning economies also entailed the ruination of the peasantry. The new landowners who "now had to enter the field with fifty, one hundred, or even more horses took everything from the poor peasants who were given to them; they took more from the peasantry in one year than the peasants had ever before paid over a period of ten years. For this reason many beautiful estates were quickly neglected and ruined just as if an enemy had passed through them."

In this general atmosphere rapacious, unscrupulous men from the bottom of society surfaced. Not infrequently they were aliens — Germans and especially Tatars who took over the positions previously held by the boyar class. This was the "democratic" idea of the Tsar's revolution and it did not escape contemporaries. "There were many of those," write Taube and Kruse — who themselves served in the *oprichnina* — "who could take the field with two hundred to three hundred horses, who had a fortune of many thousands of guldens, but who were now wandering about the country with the beggar's crutch. Others, their former slaves, who had not a single gulden, were now put in their positions on their fiefs." Another *oprichnik*, Staden, confirms this: "Now newly made lords, who should have been slaves of former lords, walk with the Grand Prince."

In short, we have here a real social revolution carried out by the sovereign power. Actually, its goal was only political: the replacement of the boyar class by a new servitor class. For the sake of this goal the country was subjected for decades to a regime of terror and destruction that encompassed all levels of society. Although Tsar Ivan did announce in January of 1565 that the business groups [*gosti*] and merchants, and all Christians were not at all in *disfavor*, in actuality the struggle with the boyar class degenerated in the very beginning into a struggle with the *zemshchina*. It should be recalled that the concept of the *zemshchina* included all classes of society, all of the old Rus' that was now placed under suspicion. The text of the oath uttered by each person entering the *oprichnina* corps has come down to us (in a German translation). In this oath one swore "not to eat, drink, or maintain friendship with the *zemshchina*." And the German *oprichnik* testifies: "Frequently it happened that if two such persons were found talking (i.e. an *oprichnik* with a member of the *zemshchina*), they were both killed regardless of the positions they held." Tsar Ivan was psychologically in a state of war with the entire Russian land. Only from the perspective of this psychology can the destruction of Novgorod, Tver' and many other cities be explained. The whole peculiarity of this civil war is that it was one-sided: the aggressive campaigns of the *oprichnina* meet with almost no opposition. The war is reduced to pogroms and to slaughter.

Let us look at the circumstances and details of this civil war as it is portrayed by contemporaries. Russian scholarship was enriched when a new source was discovered — the notes of the *oprichnik* Heinrich Staden.

In general these notes confirm the portrayal of the *oprich-nina* system by Taube and Kruse. Staden was one of the executioners of the Russian land and his naively cynical narratives of his own exploits cannot lead to suspicions of prejudice.

According to the testimony of these people, the *zemshchina* received an order from the Tsar that in affairs between members of the *zemshchina* and the *oprichnina* decisions be made in favor of the latter: "Judge fairly, so that our people be not guilty." Whether or not there was actually such an order matters little; this was obviously the way things were understood in Moscow and in all Russia. In essence, this was the abrogation of justice for one-half the country and the legalization of plunder for the other half. "It was then, as a result of this order, that the people of the *zemshchina* fell in spirit. Any member of the *oprichnina* could, for example, accuse any of the *zemshchina* that the latter owed the former a certain sum of money. And even if the member of the *zemshchina* never knew nor saw the *oprichnik*, nevertheless the accused still had to pay the *oprichnik*. Otherwise he was whipped or clubbed publicly in the market place until he paid." Staden himself tells of how he applied this system of extortion to his enemies — a German, a neighboring merchant and a wealthy peasant. The method by which, according to the description by Taube and Kruse, an *oprichnik* destroys a woman is classic. His servant gives a shirt to a neighboring house for safe-keeping and slips in a gilded goblet. Then, in the presence of an official [*tseloval'nik*], a search takes place, the merchandise is discovered, and the proprietors hauled off to court. "I was ashamed to slander this woman. In the *zemshchina* she was my close neighbor. Her first husband was an iconographer" (the second, a merchant).

This example shows that the boyars were not

the only ones who suffered from the *oprichnina*. In
Staden's stories, as in Taube's, merchants are constantly
listed among the sacrifices. Judging by the author, it could
not be otherwise since plunder and accumulation were
the chief daily interest of the *oprichnina*. Staden says
little of executions, of the brigandage at every step of
the way. When one reads Staden, it can be thought that
even Ivan the Terrible's campaign against Novgorod had
no goal other than gigantic looting. It is worthwhile to
cite his story of the Novgorod expedition, for it reveals
what was going on in all corners of the land during the
regime of the *oprichnina*.

> The Grand Prince, together with his *oprichniki*,
> robbed his own land, cities and villages, and beat
> and strangled prisoners and enemies to death. This
> is how it happened. Many carters with horses and
> sleighs were provided to take all the goods . . . from
> Novgorod to a monastery situated outside the city.
> Here everything was dumped into a pile and guarded
> so that no one could take anything away. All of
> this was supposed to have been divided fairly, but
> this did not happen. And when I saw this, I decided
> to ride no more with the Grand Prince. . .

> Then I began to take on all kinds of servants, par-
> ticularly those who were naked and barefoot. They
> were pleased with this. Later I started my own cam-
> paigns and led my people back into the country by
> another road. For this reason my people remained
> loyal to me. Every time they took anyone captive,
> they asked honorably where money, goods, and
> especially good horses could be found — in mon-
> asteries? in churches? in households? If the captive
> did not want to answer voluntarily, they tortured

him until he answered. In this way they obtained money and goods for me.

Once we approached a certain church. My people rushed inside and began to loot, grabbing icons and other such nonsense. This was not far from the court of one of the *zemshchina* princes [Staden frequently uses "prince" instead of "nobleman" — G. F.] and some three hundred armed men of the *zemshchina* had gathered there. These three hundred men were chasing six horsemen — the six were *oprichniki* whom the men of the *zemshchina* were chasing. They asked me to help and I started out after the *zemshchina*.

When they saw that so many people came out from the church, they turned back to the court. I killed one of them on the spot with a single shot; then I broke through their crowd and slipped through the gate. Stones poured down upon us from the windows of the women's quarters. Calling my servant Teshat, I quickly ran up the stairs with an axe in my hand.

The princess met me at the top of the stairs and wanted to throw herself at my feet. But, fearing my stern look, she started to rush back inside the chambers. I plunged the axe in her back and she fell on the doorstep. I stepped over the corpse and became acquainted with the women's chamber. Then we rode all night and came to a large, unprotected town. Here I did not harm anybody. I rested.

When I set out with the Grand Prince, I had one

horse. I returned with 49, of which 28 were har-
nessed to sleighs full of all kinds of goods.

The *oprichnik's* story of the Novgorod campaign
ends with the Tsar's inspection in Staritsa. It was then
that Heinrich Staden was granted the right to be called
"Andrei Vladimirovich."

> The suffix *"vich"* signifies a noble title. From
> this time on, I was made equal to princes and
> boyars. In other words, by these words the Grand
> Prince let me know that this was knighthood. In
> this nation every foreigner occupies a better position
> if, during a certain amount of time, he knows how
> to act in accordance with local customs.

Undoubtedly, Staden the German expressed this ability
fully.

Many of the *oprichnina's* feats should be ascribed
to the wilfulness of the new "knighthood." Staden himself
testifies that pillage of the *zemshchina* went on "without
the consent" of the Tsar. Many pretended to be *oprichniki*
as a cover-up for plundering. Having unbridled his army by
means of civil war, Ivan naturally could not maintain its
discipline. Besides, the cruelty and greed of those in high
positions met a similar spirit of cruelty and greed by those
from the bottom of society and it was heightened by class
spite. Let us turn again to the *oprichnik's* pen:

> Everybody slandered in order to obtain *zemshchina*
> wealth: their male and female servants, their labor-
> ers, and the commoner from the *oprichnina*, be
> he a peasant or a townsman. I pass over in silence
> that which male and female servants of *oprichnina*
> princes and gentry allowed themselves. Everything

was considered to be proper and correct because
of the decree.

The preceding words show that all excesses of lower-
class terror and plain robbery were sanctioned by the will
of the Tsar — by the whole spirit of the system created by
him. Taube and Kruse also relate that simple condescen-
sion shown by an *oprichnik* to a member of the *zemshchina* in personal affairs was viewed as treachery and
could cost him his head.

In this civil war of Tsar against *zemshchina* our
attention concerns itself with the Church. Evidently monasteries and churches particularly attracted the greed of
the *oprichnina* and of the Tsar himself. Ivan the Terrible
preferred direct robbery and destruction of churches
rather than the secularization of Church properties, the
sums of which he needed during ruinous wars. Heinrich
Staden writes: "The Grand Prince came to Tver' and
ordered us to rob everything — both churches and monasteries. The same thing happened in Torzhok. Here no
mercy was shown to a single church or monastery."

This greed for Church property, in conjunction
with the Tsar's anger at the clergy, was expressed especially clearly during the pogrom of Great Novgorod in
1571 and was described in the local chronicle. The advanced regiment of the *oprichniki* made all the necessary
preparations prior to the arrival of the Tsar.

By the sovereign's order, some boyars and lesser
gentry, who had moved to monasteries near Great
Novgorod, sealed the monasteries' clerical treasuries.
The hegumen, "black" clergy, secretaries [*d'iaki*]
and elder monks — up to five hundred elders or
more — of the Novgorod monasteries were taken by
the men of the advanced regiment to Great Nov-

gorod. Exactions were taken from all before the Tsar's arrival.

The same was done with the "white" town clergy: "It was ordered that for exaction they be beaten from morning until evening, and that twenty Novgorodian rubles be taken from each of them as the exaction." Arrests were also made among the boyars and merchants of Novgorod, but exactions were not taken from them. The next day, upon his arrival in Novgorod on Janurary 7, the Tsar ordered all the monks exacted or else "to be clubbed to death, and, after being beaten, taken to their own monasteries for burial." Only on the following day did the general pillaging and executions in Novgorod begin. The Tsar sought his first victims among the monks.

In his *"History"* Prince Kurbskii devotes a special chapter (VIII) to "the suffering of religious martyrs." As his other chapters, this one also is not free from inaccuracies. But some facts are confirmed by the chronicles and by Ivan the Terrible's own *Sinodik* — i.e. a memorial of his sacrifices sent by the Tsar to various monasteries. Kurbskii writes the following about the murder of Kornilii, hegumen of the Pecherskii Monastery in Pskov, and about the murder of his pupil, Vassian Muromtsev. "And, it is said, they were crushed together by an instrument of torture on the same day. Their bodies were also buried together like holy martyrs." Kurbskii vaguely mentions, without indicating the name, the murder of Leonid, Archbishop of Novgorod and Pimen's successor: "and he ordered the great hegumen and archimandrite to be killed." The *Chronicle of Pskov* reports the details of the unheard of execution of the archbishop: "Tsar Ivan Vasil'evich was angry at Archbishop Leonid of Novgorod. He took him to Moscow, de-frocked him, dressed him in bear skin and set the dogs upon him." Like Kurbskii,

we cannot check the reports about Ivan's murder of
Feodorit, the famous "enlightener" of the Lapps. According to some rumors, the Tsar drowned him because
he had petitioned that Kurbskii, who was once his spiritual
son, be forgiven. The Tsar's *Sinodik* gives us the names
of other "monks" also, of "priests," and even "elder
nuns" who will probably never be identified. But the
Sinodik, too, is far from being complete. Suffice it to
say that St. Filipp's name is not in it.

The executions of the clergy may have been brought
about by the Tsar's greed or by suspicion of the participation of the Church's representatives in the alleged
crimes of the *zemshchina*. If so, then they were but a
detail in the *oprichnina's* regime. But these executions
could also be the vengeance of a tyrant who was irritated
by words of admonition and by the moral curb which he
received from only a few priests. We cannot, of course,
see these executions as the expression of the Tsar's anti-
Christian or anti-ecclesiastical ideas. Ivan was able to
combine the executions of priests and even his hatred of
priests with a consciousness of being a defender of Orthodoxy. He enjoyed theological debate, especially with
foreigners; he was an assiduous reader of Holy Scripture;
he was a specialist in the *Typikon*; and he was not only a
defender of the faith but also of piety. This faith, however,
was expressed by him in forms that were abominable
atrocities. The beauty of the liturgy evoked a sense of
excitement in Ivan which incited in him a craving for the
shedding of human blood, just as the excitement of
voluptuousness also incited him in this same direction.
Because the question of the *oprichnina's* hoods and the
Tsar's clothes play a certain — perhaps excessively large —
role in the clash between the Metropolitan and the Tsar,
we feel it necessary to look at that blasphemous parody
of monastic brotherhood which the Tsar created in the

depths of the *oprichnina*.

The Tsar's court — and it was a select corps of executioners in the Aleksandrovskii settlement — consisted of three hundred persons — "brothers" — at whose head stood the Tsar with the rank of hegumen, Prince Viazemskii as treasurer, and Maliuta Skuratov as ecclesiarch. The *oprichniki* wore black cloaks above their caftans and hoods on their heads, all of which in external appearance reminded people of monks — an original idea for a spiritual-police order! The hegumen woke the brethren during the night and forced them to stand in church from twelve until three in the morning. During the quite lavish dinner, the Tsar read from the *Lives of the Saints*. Orders for executions, together with details of torture, were frequently given in church. Arising from the table, the Tsar "hardly ever skipped a day of going into the torture chamber." The sight of torture "by his very nature gave him a special joy and comfort. He was never so happy in countenance and in speech as when he was present during tortures and executions. He executes before the eight o'clock bell" which called people to evening prayer. The strict and orderly regulation of the custom of this ecclesiastical-torture chamber destroys the common interpretation and understanding of Ivan the Terrible's religiosity — that is, that it was a state of radical vacillation between sin and repentance. Without rejecting the Tsar's repentant moods, it is impossible not to see that within his daily routine he was able to combine atrocity with religious piety and thus he profaned the very idea of an Orthodox realm.

What has been said above should be enough to convince us that it is quite erroneous to view the *oprichnina* as an expedient governmental institution which was directed solely against a rebellious boyar class. It is therefore also erroneous to interpret St. Filipp's struggle with

Ivan the Terrible as merely the voice of that same boyar opposition.

Those Russians who wrote about the *oprichnina* as contemporaries of Ivan the Terrible and those who wrote thereafter are unanimous in their indignation. Not one voice was found in its defense. The renowned Ivan Peresvetov, in whom many have seen the ideologue of the *oprichnina*, wrote long before the bloody years and it is difficult to judge whether he would have been pleased with what he wrote if he had lived to encounter the bloody years. We will cite just some of the testimony from the voices of chroniclers and "reporters."

> In God's punishment for our sins, Tsar Ivan Vasil'-evich became infuriated with all Orthodoxy. . . At the advice of evil men . . . he instituted the *oprichnina*, divided the cities and the land . . . and it was difficult. There was hatred for the Tsar in the world and many executions took place.
> (*Sokrashchennyi Vremennik*).

Prince Katyrev-Rostovskii in *The Tale of Time of Troubles* [*Povest' o smutnom vremeni*] gives a clear and precise characteristic of the *oprichnina*: "For the increase of sins of all Orthodox Christianity, Tsar Ivan Vasil'evich, the enemy, having become full of wrath and fury, began to subject his subordinates — slaves in essence — to evil and began to persecute them unmercifully and to spill their blood. And he divided his realm, entrusted to him by God, into two parts . . . and he commanded those in his "part" to coerce the members of the other part and to put them to death and to rob their homes. He ordered innocent commanders [*voevody*], entrusted to him by God, to be killed. And he had no fear of ecclesiastic rank, killing some and incarcerating others. He ordered the most beautiful cities of Novgorod and Pskov to be destroyed. And he evilly and unmercifully killed Orthodox Christians in these cities, including infants."

Even the *d'iak* Ivan Timofeev, author of the chronicle *"Vremennik,"* tries to pass over the "Tsar's outrageous style of daily life" in silence. It is only by cleverly selecting his words that he bares the "coldness of the crown" and depicts the *oprichnina* with sharp and decisive expressions: "The Tsar began to hate the cities of his land" and in his anger he divided his people "creating a situation similar to that of dual allegiance." All contemporaries were especially depressed by the "division" of the realm — by that which constituted the very essence of the *oprichnina* and against which, on the eve of his election, Metropolitan Filipp raised his voice.

CHAPTER FIVE

ST. FILIPP AND
IVAN THE TERRIBLE

In the winter of 1567-1568 the Tsar returned from the unsuccessful Lithuanian campaign. A storm was gathering over Moscow. The letters from King Sigismund and hetman Khotkevich to the Moscow boyars were intercepted and served as a cause for executions. The letters were addressed to Princes Bel'skii, Mstislavskii, Vorotynskii and to the equerry, the boyar Ivan Petrovich Cheliadnin. The boyars were invited to leave the sovereign-tyrant and cross over to Lithuania. This invitation to treason met with no success. The boyars, probably at the Tsar's bidding, wrote insulting replies to Lithuania which have come down to us. Cheliadnin wrote the following to the King: "I am already old. Were I to betray my sovereign, it would be like breaking my heart, and I then could not live for long. Were I with you, I could no longer be in your armed forces . . . and I have not been trained to be a jester." In his letter to the hetman he refers to the Russian sovereign and his service in this way: "And concerning what I may have written — that my sovereign wanted to shed my blood — this could not be . . . It cannot be that the Tsar's majesty would punish me without my being guilty. And it was never the case that Lithuania could judge Moscow."

These letters, however, did not save the boyar. We do not know why — of all the persons to whom King

Sigismund wrote — only Cheliadnin was executed. The fact that Bel'skii and the others were not touched indicates that there was no conspiracy. Perhaps the Tsar was taking revenge on Cheliadnin for past "sins," for participating, according to Solov'ev's supposition, in a revolt twenty one years earlier against the Glinskiis. He was already quite old and, in the words of the *oprichnik* Staden who knew him personally, had the reputation of being the only honest judge in Moscow. One contemporary foreigner relates the tragic and mocking circumstances of Cheliadnin's murder. Ivan allegedly dressed him in Tsar's clothing and put the crown on him. He placed him on the throne and bowed, calling him the "Tsar" of the Russian land. Then he stabbed him in the heart with a knife. The *oprichniki* then killed the old man and dragged the body out of the Court, throwing it into the square. Staden notes laconically: "he was killed and thrown into a manure pile near the Neglinna River."

Cheliadnin's wife also perished with him. The Tsar's hatred for the Cheliadnin family was so great that, according to unanimous testimony, he slaughtered their servants and livestock and burned down their estates so that nothing would be left alive. This was the beginning of a new flare-up of terror. It appears that a treasonous affair was concocted around Cheliadnin, an affair in which many of the boyar families allegedly participated. It was then that Princes I. A. Kurakin-Bulgakov, D. Riapolovskii, and the three Rostovskii princes perished. About one of them, who had served as a commander [*voevoda*] in Nizhnii-Novgorod, it is related that the Tsar's envoys — the *oprichniki* — seized him in church and beheaded him on the road to Moscow. His head was given to the Tsar. Some of the victims of the Tsar's "*disfavor*" — such as Prince Shcheniatev and Prince Turuntai-Pronskii — thought they could save their lives by renouncing the world and becoming monks. But the monastic cloak did not save them. According to one source, they were beaten to death with rods. Kurbskii writes that the Tsar ordered Pronskii to be drowned and Shcheniatev to be subjected to horrible torture in the monastery — "to be burned on a metal pan and have needles driven under his nails, And he died of these tortures." The treasurer, Kh. Iu. Tiutin, his wife, two young sons and two daughters perished along with the boyars. If we are to believe the German *oprichnik*, the treasurer was sliced to pieces by Mikhail Temriukovich, the Tsar's own brother-in-law. If all the details of the executions are trustworthy, they do not constitute the improbable. Political executions were already turning to slaughter.

Did only the representatives of famous families tremble during this period of the Tsar's fury? Taube and Kruse describe these months of terror: "It was a pitiful and sorrowful spectacle of slaughter and killings. Every day ten, twenty or more *oprichniki*, with arms concealing large axes under their cloaks, rode about the streets and alleys. Each detachment had its own list of boyars, *d'iaki*, princes and leading merchants. No one knew what his own guilt or alleged wrongdoing was supposed to be. No one knew the hour of his own death or even the fact that he had been condemned. All would go about their usual affairs as if nothing was the matter. Suddenly a band of killers would descend on them — whether in the street, by the gates, or in the market — and the killers chopped and choked them without making any accusation — without any trial — and then they threw out their corpses. And not one person dared to bury the corpses." We omit other terrible, and perhaps exaggerated, details of these bloody days. That corpses of the murdered did lie about for days in the streets is confirmed by the German *oprichnik* Staden.

This raging violence of the terror of the *oprichnina* falls over the winter and spring of 1568. A more accurate chronology of events is not possible. It was then that the reproachful voice of Filipp sounded before the Tsar for the first time.

Filipp's *Life* narrates that "certain of the magnates and the people" came to their pastor in tears, begging him to intercede: "he saw death in front of his eyes and, having been shown this suffering, he could not but speak." With the spectacle of so many villainous acts and so much suffering, the hierarch could remain silent no longer. He made use of his right of intercession [*pechalovanie*] , a right recently recognized again by the Tsar. His first discussions with and admonitions to Ivan the Terrible occurred in private. Filipp's *Life* cites one of these discussions with the Tsar. It is valuable to us not as an exact transcript of the hierarch's words but as an ideal dialogue between the spiritual leader of the Church and the Tsar of the secular realm. This type of ideal was deeply expressive of Muscovite religious consciousness in the sixteenth century.

— O Sovereign, said Filipp, you possess a rank higher than all honor, almost that of God who gave you this dignity, for the worldly scepter is only the likeness of the heavenly . . . Adhere to God's law which is given to you and rule lawfully in the world. The possession of worldly riches is to be likened to river waters, for it is gradually depleted. Only the heavenly treasure of truth is preserved. If you are high in rank, then in body you are just like any other man, for though you may be honored with God's image, you are still God's "subject." He who truly can be called a ruler, rules himself, he is not controlled by passions

but is victorious over passions through love. . .
Has it ever been heard that pious Tsars themselves
antagonize their state? . . .

— What do you, monk, need in our royal councils?
Or do you not know that my people wish to devour
me?

— Do not deceive yourself with pointless fear. By
the election of the holy council and with your
approval I became the pastor of Christ's Church
and we are all at one with you in maintaining the
piety and salvation of all Orthodox Christianity.

— I repeat only one thing to you, honest father:
be silent and bless us as we desire.

— Our silence places a sin on your soul and causes
death throughout the land. If one of a ship's at-
tendants falls into temptation, he does not cause
great misfortune to the voyagers. But if the helmsman falls, he brings the entire ship to ruin. If we
are to follow human will, how shall we be able to
say on the day of the coming of the Lord: these
are my children whom Thou hast entrusted to
me? Did not the Lord himself command in the
Gospel that one can have no greater love than that
one lay down his life for his friends, and that if you
dwell in love, you will truly be my disciples? Thus
we think and we hold to this firmly.

— Holy Father, my friends and sincere allies have
revolted against me and I now grieve as did holy
David of old: "My friends have forsaken me. Let
them be put to shame and dishonor who seek after

my life!"

— Sovereign, there are people who speak cunningly to you. Accept good counsel, not flattery. Do not divide your realm, for you have been placed by God to judge God's people in truth, not to take the image of a torturer upon yourself. All that is in the world passes away — both honor and glory. Only life in God is immortal. When all that is earthly is removed, then we will have to give an account of our lives to God. Remove all the slanderers from you as though rotten limbs and make your people one, for God is only present where there is the spirit of oneness and the spirit of sincere love.

— Filipp, do not contradict our authority lest my wrath fall upon you. If you persist, step down from your ecclesiastical position.

— I did not entreat you nor did I solicit, nor did I bribe anyone in order to obtain this ecclesiastical power. Why did you deprive me of the hermitage and of the holy fathers? If you dare act contrary to the canons, then do anything you wish. But I must not weaken when the time of encounter comes.

Such were these private discussions with the Tsar. But they had no success. It may be thought that Filipp did not have much influence on the Tsar after the arguments about the *oprichnina* which took place during his election. The Tsar clearly kept away from the hierarch and avoided encounters with him. In the admonitions of Metropolitan Filipp the Tsar seemed to hear that same hateful voice of the seditious boyars. Metropolitan

Filipp spoke out ever more energetically and strictly. According to Kurbskii, he "first began his entreaties by speaking on many occasions but he then threatened that if the Tsar did not listen, the Tsar would then become a victim of the last judgment of Christ. And Filipp so threatened in accordance with the episcopal power given to him by God."

Only when he became convinced of the fruitlessness of private admonitions did Filipp bring his great controversy with the Tsar to the nation so that the matter could be judged. His first clash with Ivan in the Cathedral of the Assumption created such an impression on his contemporaries that the distant Novgorod chronicler observed in his sparse notes: "On March 22, during the fourth week of the Veneration of the Cross, Metropolitan Filipp began to quarrel with the sovereign about the *oprichnina*." We have illustrations of this famous dialogue in the cathedral between the hierarch and the Tsar in Filipp's *Life* and in the narrative by the German *oprichniki* who wrote four years after the events. It is remarkable that these sources, so distant and independent, so different in character and style, transmit in the same way the idea of Filipp's speeches. This is proof of the deep impression that these speeches left on a Muscovite society which preserved them for tens of years in the form of *oral tradition*. In his account, Karamzin could easily blend the Slavonic phrases from the *Lives* with the German translations of Taube and Kruse. And in his skillful merger he created a classic page of Russian national history. Unfortunately, too much in these memorable words belongs to the eloquent pen of the historian. It would be more cautious of us to give both versions separately.

According to the *Life*, the Tsar came to the cathedral on Sunday "dressed in black robes" and in the company of his *oprichnina*. They wore high hoods over their heads "like Chaldean boors." St. Filipp was presumably happy at the Tsar's arrival, "taking on a divine light." Three times the Tsar approached Metropolitan Filipp but the hierarch said not a word. The boyars then exclaimed: "Holy Metropolitan! Tsar Ivan Vasil'evich demands your blessing." Glancing at the Tsar, blessed Filipp said:

> Devout one, of whom have you become so jealous that it forces you to change the beauty of your face? From the time that the sun has begun to shine in the sky it has been unheard of that devout Tsars disturb the peace of their realm. Fear God's judgment and be ashamed of your own imperial robes. If you impose laws on others, why do you then yourself commit acts which are worthy of condemnation? The God-inspired chronicler spoke truthfully: loathe words of flattery because the dispositions of flatterers are more rapacious than those of ravens. Ravens only pluck out physical eyes but flatterers blind the soul's vision and the soul's thoughts by praising that which deserves vilification and by condemning that which is worthy of praise. Desist from such undertakings — such things are not characteristic of your pious realm. How much do Orthodox Christians suffer! We, O Sovereign, have a pure and bloodless sacrifice to God which is for the salvation of man, but outside the altar Christian blood is being shed and people are dying needlessly. Or have you forgotten that you also are of this earth and also need the forgiveness of your sins? Forgive and you will be forgiven, for it is only through the forgiveness of our fellow creatures that we shall escape the Lord's wrath. You have studied Holy Scripture in depth.

Why do you not show some zeal and respect for
Scripture? Whoever does not love his brother or
is not truthful is not of God.

The Tsar flew into a rage:

— Filipp, do you wish to test our good will? It is
better for you if you are in accord with us.

— But then, O Sovereign, our faith will be in vain
and the apostolic message will be in vain. And the
holy traditions of our holy fathers will be of no
avail. Even all the good deeds which flow from
Christian teaching will be pointless. And the very
Incarnation of our Lord who became man for the
sake of our salvation will be in vain if we now
drop that which God has entrusted to us so that
we can be in accord with this immorality. And this
will not be! God will punish you for all of this, for
it has brought about division in the realm. I do
not grieve for those who innocently are shedding
their blood and are dying as martyrs because this
present, temporary suffering — in the words of the
apostles — is nothing compared with that glory
which will be revealed in us. But for your salvation
I do grieve.

Ivan struck the crozier against the rostrum of the
cathedral and pronounced threateningly:

— Are you an enemy of our authority? We shall
see what your strength is.

— Sovereign, I cannot obey your command rather
than God's. The land and its fulfillment belong to

God. Just as my predecessors, I too am only a
stranger and a migrant on earth. I will pursue
the truth of piety even though I lose my rank
and suffer cruelly as a result of my action.

The German authors present Metropolitan Filipp's
speech in the following manner:

— All merciful Tsar and Grand Prince, how long
do you wish to shed the innocent blood of your
loyal Christian people. How long will falsehood
reign in the Russian realm? Tatars and pagans —
and the whole world — would claim that all nations
have law and truth but not Rus'. All over the world
there are criminals who seek mercy from rulers
and find it, but there is no mercy in Rus' for the
innocent and the righteous. Realize that even
though God has elevated you in this world, you
are still a mortal man and God will inflict punishment on you for the innocent blood which is being
shed. The stones under your feet, if not living souls,
will cry out and will accuse and judge you. By
God's command I must tell you this even though
death befall me as a result.

These words, continue the authors, brought the
Tsar to terrible fury. He struck the floor with his crozier
and replied: "Until now I have been humble before you,
Metropolitan, and I have been humble with your followers
and with my realm. Now you shall come to know me!"
And with this threat he left the church.

Executions commenced anew on the following
day. This time the Tsar's wrath fell upon the boyars and
the servitors [*sluzhilye liudi*] of the metropolitan's court.
Many of them were seized and subjected to horrible

tortures; such torture was probably an attempt to elicit
some type of contrived evidence against Filipp. Slander,
instigated by fear, was about to sting the hierarch. This
we shall observe later.

Moscow lived the summer of 1568 in fear. All
contemporaries speak of the Tsar's savage and punitive
expedition against the outlying Muscovite villages. Taube
and Kruse give the day of departure (the 9th or the 19th
of June) and the length (six weeks) of this campaign.
Whether the target had been the estates of Cheliadnin
alone or of other boyars as well, the *oprichnina* army
burned all the buildings, annihilated the people and
livestock and subjected the women to unheard of outrage.
If we are to believe the German authors, the Tsar seized
women from the homes of Moscow boyars, *d'iaki* and
merchants. He and his army violated them and then
ordered them to be taken back to their homes, to their
husbands. Many of them committed suicide. One detail
of this story, repeated in Staden's sparing words, lends
credence to it. All authors speak of women and young
girls who were stripped naked and forced to chase chickens
for the amusement of the Tsar and the *oprichnina*.

Prince Kurbskii connects the death of one of the
Kolychovs, Ivan Borisovich, the nephew of Metropolitan
Filipp, with this summer campaign. This story, however,
is not the easiest to believe. Kurbskii himself speaks of
a "miracle" but adds that he heard of it "from an eyewitness, furthermore from a perceptive one." In any case,
the story is as follows. When the Tsar was burning Ivan
Petrovich's (Cheliadnin's) villages, he ordered the young
Kolychov to be tied "in the very uppermost chambers"
of a certain house. The entire house, just like the neighboring houses, was packed with people. Several barrels
of gunpowder were rolled up to the house and ignited.
Ivan Kolychov was found far away in a field with a hand

tied to a log, but alive. One of the *oprichniki* cut off his head with a sword. The Tsar ordered his head to be sewn in leather and sent to his uncle, Metropolitan Filipp, "incarcerated in prison," with the words: "This is the head of your kinsman. Your sorcery did not help him." The mention of prison is an obvious anachronism because Filipp was still free. At the beginning of his open controversy with the Tsar, he moved from the house of the metropolitanate (in the Kremlin) to the Monastery of Nikolai the Elder. If the monastery is not the "dungeon," then the famous scene of the sending of Ivan Kolychov's head, in accordance with the *Life*, must be placed several months later — to the days following Metropolitan Filipp's removal on the eighth of November. But perhaps the executions of the Kolychovs really did not begin during the summer. Kurbskii writes that there were almost ten of them, adults and servitors of course: "and the relatives were destroyed." Ivan the Terrible's *Sinodik* mentions four Kolychovs. That not all of them perished upon Metropolitan Filipp's "*disfavor*" is seen from a list of boyars in which, under the year 7079 (1571), it is noted: "The courtier [*okol'nichii*] Mikhailo Ivanovich Kolychov quit."

The second public encounter between Tsar and Metropolitan, as noted in the *Life*, took place during the summer atrocities. This was on the twenty-eighth of July, the day of the apostles Prokhor and Nikanor. On that day Filipp was participating in a liturgical service in the Novodevichii Monastery. The Tsar and his boyars came. At the end of the religious procession around the walls of the monastery, Metropolitan Filipp reached the holy gates where he was to read from the Gospel. Glancing back, he saw one of the Tsar's retainers standing "with a cap on." Just as in the Cathedral of the Assumption, this detail of the clothing of the *oprichnina* gave cause for accusation. "Sovereign Tsar," said Filipp, "is this the way the pious are to behave?" Are they to uphold Islamic law? (i.e. standing at prayer with hats on, as is the Islamic custom). The Tsar responded: "How so?" And Metropolitan Filipp answered: "There he is, one of your guards who came in with you, the one who looks like Satan." The Tsar looked back but the guilty one had already removed his hat. Despite the Tsar's questions, no one betrayed the *oprichnik*. Ivan became furious, reviled the hierarch, cursed him as a liar, a mutineer and a scoundrel.

These clashes were not the only ones. According to the *Life*, not one meeting between Tsar and Metropolitan went without altercation: "whenever they met, the words uttered were not peaceful." It was then that Ivan the Terrible decided to remove the recalcitrant hierarch. He dared not to deal with him in the same way he dealt with the boyars. Ivan had not yet had the occasion to kill bishops. He sought legal pretext for his pre-meditated violence. The policy during the reign of both Ivan the Terrible and his father was that hierarchs whom the Tsars did not appreciate removed themselves from office and retired to monasteries. The courageous Filipp did not consider it possible to leave his flock and the service entrusted to him by God. And had he not even obliged himself to the earthly Tsar in 1566 that he would "not leave the metropolitanate"? The Tsar planned to convene a council to try Metropolitan Filipp; that is, to disguise the coercive removal of Filipp in canonical form. He was easily able to find men in the upper hierarchy who would be willing to meet him halfway. The demoralizing effect of terror was obviously one of the reasons some hierarchs were ready to participate in the transgression which was being planned in the name of the Church. Filipp's *Life* clearly characterizes the disposition of clerical opportunists who were dissatisfied from the very beginning with Filipp's courageous accusations. The following words are attributed to those who were "obsequious" to the Tsar: "It would be good for you to listen to the Tsar in everything and to bless all his undertakings without any discourse, and to do his will and not to be angry. Appease his anger and thereby change it to mercy." From St. Filipp's *Life* we discover that among the hierarchy there was an entire "faction" which was hostile to him: "Accomplices in this evil were Pimen of Novgorod, Pafnutii of Suzdal', Filofei of Riazan' and the archpriest Evstafii . . ." We know the reason for Evstafii's animosity toward Filipp — Metropolitan Filipp had reproached him for his "spiritual dealings as father-confessor of the Tsar." We may surmise that the guilt of Evstafii was that he was too lenient with the sins of his spiritual son. Evstafii became the Tsar's main instigator and intriguer against Filipp. We know nothing of the reasons for the bishops' animosity toward Filipp. The *Life* does mention, however, that Pimen, an ambitious and the most important hierarch of the Russian Church after the metropolitan, dreamed of "taking his throne." About the majority, who were intimidated and servile, the words of the *Life* express it quite well: "The others were advocates neither of Filipp nor of the Tsar, but merely did as the Tsar wished."

What charges were brought against the Saint? Taube and Kruse, well informed on the Filipp affair, state that the Tsar "called forth false witnesses against the Pope" (that is their term for the "Metropolitan") who testified that Filipp "allegedly leads an unseemly and indecorous life." The scene in the Cathedral of the Assumption, as described in the *Life*, is connected with Filipp's accusatory speech. The Tsar and the bishops were still in the Cathedral when the reader ["*anagnost*"] of the Cathedral Church, taught by Filipp's enemies, began to "speak evil against the blessed one." The bishops who played up to the Tsar, such as Pimen of Novgorod and others, said: "How can you admonish the Tsar when you yourself act violently?" The Saint replied to Pimen: "Even though you are obsequious and endeavor to take another's throne, you will soon be overthrown from your own." To the reader Filipp said: "May Christ be merciful to you, gentle one."

For other false witnesses the Tsar turned to the Solovetskii Monastery. An investigative commission was sent to the island. It consisted of three persons: the bishop of Suzdal', Pafnutii; the archimandrite of the Andronikovskii Monastery, Feodosii; and Prince Vasilii Temkin. The commission acted by means of intimidation and temptation. We may accept the *Life's* defense of the monastery when it claims that the majority were neither intimidated nor tempted. But a group of traitors was found, including hegumen Paisii who had just recently sent presents to Metropolitan Filipp in Moscow. It is said that Paisii was promised the rank of bishop. We do not know what evidence the Solovetskii witnesses could give, but they played the major role at the council.

According to some of Kurbskii's allusions — the words he places on Ivan's lips — it may be thought that here too things did not go without the accusation of sorcery, an accusation which was common in the political trials of the time. We hear nothing of that which touches upon purely political charges; that is, participation in boyar plots. Evidently the members of the council limited themselves to faults of a strictly ecclesiastical nature.

The council met for the mock trial in Moscow in the beginning of November. According to Kurbskii, it took place in the "great church", that is, in the Cathedral of the Assumption. The righteous hierarch of Kazan' was no longer among the living. In addition to Herman, Elevferii of Suzdal', the one who had once refused to sign Filipp's statement about the *oprichnina*, had also died. Not a word of truth could be expected from either side. The holy confessor had to drink the entire bitter cup — he was to be accused by a council of the Russian Church rather than by the capriciousness of the arbitrary tyrant; he was to be defamed by his spiritual children. Heading the group from the Solovetskii Monastery, Paisii presented "rolls" of testimony from Solovki. These accusations were read before the council. St. Filipp replied humbly to his slanderer: "May God's grace be on your lips, child, for flattery has been warded off from me. Have you not heard God's word — whoever calls his brother a fool is guilty of the judgment. Recall another statement from Holy Scripture — whatever a man sows that shall he also reap. These are not my words but are the words of God." According to the *Life*, Filipp's last words to the Tsar were:

Desist, O Sovereign, from such profane deeds. Recall former Tsars. Remember that those who did good are kindly remembered after death, but that those who did evil to their realm are no longer held in reverence. You too should attempt to imitate good morals. You must remember that your high earthly rank has no control over death which sinks its invincible teeth into everything. And thus, before death's unmerciful coming, cultivate the fruits of a virtuous man and store up your treasure in heaven. For everything gathered in this world remains here. And remember that each must answer for his own life.

According to Taube and Kruse, Filipp, having fin-

ished his speech, wanted to take off his hierarch's vestments and depart. But the Tsar forced him to put them
on again and not to remove them until the court had
reached a decision. On the following day, St.
Michael's Day, Filipp, as still the canonical metropolitan, had to
celebrate the liturgy in the cathedral. Filipp consented.
Evidently, the sentence against Filipp was passed in his
absence. The same authors write that the Tsar insisted
on a death sentence (by burning) for Metropolitan Filipp,
but that the clergy pleaded for the life of Filipp and they
were ultimately successful. Death by fire again points
to the charge of sorcery. Metropolitan Filipp was condemned to being removed from his rank and he was
then incarcerated in a monastery. Neither the council's
sentence nor its motives have been preserved. The Tsar,
perhaps sparing Filipp's life against his will, was able
to create a cruel and dramatic setting for the carrying
out of the sentence.

On the eighth of November, the feast day of St.
Michael, St. Filipp was standing in front of the altar
preparing to celebrate his last liturgy. At this time Aleksei
Basmanov walked into the church with a group of *oprichniki*. In his hands was a scroll. Loudly he read the council's
decision depriving Filipp of the rank of bishop. The
oprichniki then jumped on Filipp and began to tear
his robes from him. The *Life* gives his last prophetic
words to the shaken people: "Children, sorrowful is
this separation but I am happy that I have gained this
for the Church. The time of its widowhood has come,
for its pastors, like hired hands, will be despised. They
will not maintain their pulpit and they will not be buried
in their Cathedral Church of the Mother of God." In
addition, the *oprichniki* dressed the hierarch in crude
monk's clothing which was "much sewn and torn" and,
placing him on a sled, took him dishonorably from the

Kremlin, cursing and hitting him with brooms. In tears
the people saw their pastor off. The Saint gave his blessing
to the people. He was brought to the Bogoiavlenskii
Monastery . . . where the first dungeon was earmarked
for him. Consoling the loyal flock, Filipp made his last
exhortation to them:

> I have taken all this for your good so that your
> trouble will be pacified. If it was not for my love
> for you, I would not have wanted to remain here
> for even a day. But God's word held me: a good
> shepherd gives up his life for his sheep. Do not be
> disturbed. All this discord is from the devil but
> God, who has permitted it, is our helper. Christ
> is with us, whom are we to fear? I am ready to
> suffer, for you and your love will weave a crown
> for me in the next world. Victory is accompanied
> by pain, but I beg you, do not abandon hope.
> God punishes us but with love and also for the
> good of our redemption. Our wounds are not
> from foreigners but from our own people. Bear
> grief from them joyously, for God has commanded
> that we do good to those who hate us. Pray for
> them. God in his kindness will bring everything
> to a good purpose in this world.

From the Bogoiavlenskii Monastery Filipp was once
more summoned to appear before the council for the
triumphant pronouncement of the sentence. On the
eleventh of November, two days after Filipp's deposition,
Kirill, the archimandrite of Holy Trinity Monastery, was
elevated to the metropolitan's throne. Pimen's ambitious
hopes, if he actually nurtured them, were deceived. A few
days later St. Filipp was transferred to the Nikol'skii
Monastery where he was bound in fetters like a common

prisoner. Prince Kurbskii, in depicting the gloomy condition of his imprisonment, tells of Ivan the Terrible's
attempts to destroy the Saint in the very first days after
the trial.

He commanded him to be tied hand, foot and hip
with the heaviest chains and had him thrown into
a narrow and dark dungeon. And this was shut
with strong rivets and locks and guards were also
stationed by the dungeon. Then after a day or
two, he sent his retainers to the dungeon to see
if Filipp was dead. And they said they saw Filipp
freed from those heavy fetters with his hands on
the *Psalter* and the fetters were lying beside him.
The messengers cried and fell to their knees . . .
and they told the bloodthirsty one (the Tsar)
what they had seen. And he said: "my traitor has
performed sorcery, sorcery!" The Tsar then ordered
a fierce bear, which had been starved, to be put
in Filipp's dungeon and locked in (this was heard
from an eyewitness). In the morning the Tsar
himself came and ordered the dungeon to be opened
— and he saw him unharmed, standing at prayer.
The beast was lying in the corner as humble as
a sheep.

Filipp's *Life* reports nothing of these miracles and the
attempts on his life. Taube and Kruse write that the Tsar
ordered that four coins [*altyny*] per day be allotted for
the upkeep of the prisoner.

   In contrast to Kurbskii, the *Life* ascribes to these
days of Moscow imprisonment the tragic episode in which
the head of one of the Kolychov's was sent to Filipp.
"This is your beloved relative. Your sorcery did not help
him." Filipp took the head, bowed to the ground, kissed

the head and said: "Blessed are you that God has chosen and taken you. Eternal be your memory, from generation to generation." The *Life* errs only in calling it the head of Filipp's brother Mikhail Ivanovich. The courtier [*okol'-nichii*] Mikhail Ivanovich Kolychov was executed only in 1571.

Persecuted by the Tsar and betrayed by the clergy, the holy sufferer could only find solace in the people's love. A crowd never left the gates of the Nikol'skii Monastery, the place of Filipp's incarceration. People tried to catch a glimpse of the prisoner's cell. His last words were passed on from one person to another. The Tsar decided to remove his still dangerous enemy farther from Moscow. The Otroch' Monastery in Tver' was chosen. During the move to Tver' the attempt was made to make things as painful as possible. According to the *Life*, "on the way the Saint suffered from much obscenity and abasement, riding on mules and being denied necessities." The suffering Saint also had to bear much from the appointed guard, the "ungrateful police official" ["*pristav*"] whose name history has preserved for us: his name was Stepan Kobylin.

Here in Tver' days of cramped imprisonment, warmed by the flame of prayer, dragged on for the Saint. Whatever Filipp's rank or function — whether as a monk, as a prior of a monastery, or as the pastor of and intercessor for the whole Russian land — Filipp proved himself to be Christ's true servant and soon the voice which was beckoning had to be heard: "Enter into the joy of your Lord God." Another year of silence was granted to him for his last cleansing. All that was wordly and passionate was being purged through incessant prayer. His *Life* attempts to illuminate his supplication before God with words from Holy Scripture. "Who shall separate us from the love of Christ? Shall tribulation, or distress, or per-

secution, or famine, or nakedness, or peril, or sword? . . .
For thy sake we are being killed all the day long; we
are regarded as sheep to be slaughtered. Glory to God's
name unto ages of ages."

Meanwhile the storm continued to rage over all
of Rus'. Freed from any moral constraint from the power
of the Church, Ivan decided on a crime that perhaps
may have been politically tempting to him for a long
time — the murder of his cousin, Prince Andrei Vladimirovich Staritskii, with whose kin the fate of the Kolychovs was intertwined more than once in the sixteenth
century. The Prince perished (he was poisoned) with his
wife and his whole family only two months after Filipp's
deposition (on the sixth of January of 1569). The new
metropolitan said nothing. Added to the calamities of
the *oprichnina* and the horror of war was the intensification of the plague. People fled from long inhabited
places, places which had now been ravaged by the *oprichnina*. Villages and towns were becoming deserted. At
this time the civil war between Tsar and people took
on new forms. Entire cities were marked for destruction
and slaughter. In December of 1569 all towns between
Moscow and Novgorod were subjected to the pogrom.
This was a true military conquest in the manner of the
sixteenth century. It was the conquest of one's own
land whose people had no thought of revolt or resistance.
The contrived charge against Novgorod was that this
city's rulers were allegedly preparing to go over to the
Polish king. But what could be put forth as the guilt of
Klin, Tver', Vyshnii Volochek and other towns which
happened to be in the way of the Tsar's army? We have
given already a description of several scenes from this
campaign from the viewpoint of an *oprichnik* who participated in it. Motives of plunder predominate here.
But for the Tsar the motive may have been revenge against

"unseen" enemies.

The killings began already in Klin. Taube and Kruse write that in this town Ivan met a large party of 470 families from Pskov, families which were being driven to Moscow by Ivan's decree in order to settle in those areas of the city devastated by the plague. These people were killed along with the inhabitants of Klin. The raiding horde approached Tver'. Ivan did not enter the town but stopped at one of the nearest monasteries. At the Tsar's command the forces began to rob the town, selecting the clergy as their first victims. They burned what they could not take and tortured and killed people. The foreigners particularly note the tragic fate of the Lithuanian prisoners who were locked up in the towers of the fortress. They were all killed or drowned in ice-holes. In this bloody confusion the Tsar remembered the Tver' prisoner and sent Maliuta Skuratov to Filipp's cell. The *oprichnik's* order was to request St. Filipp's blessing for the Novgorod campaign! It is natural to assume that Maliuta had another, secret order or else he well guessed the Tsar's thoughts. Otherwise he perhaps would not have dared to do what he did or could not have remained unpunished.

It is told that the martyr had already had a presentiment of his death and predicted it to those around him. "The time for my death has drawn near." On the very day of his death he received the Holy Eucharist.

On the twenty-third of December the Tsar's messenger entered Filipp's cell. No one was a witness of what occurred. The *Life* of Filipp describes his death in the following manner. Maliuta turned to him with the words: "Holy Bishop, give your blessing to the Tsar for his expedition to Great Novgorod." Perceiving his true thought, Filipp replied: "Do what you wish and do what you came to do, my friend." Then Filipp opened his arms to the

Lord with the words of his last prayer: "Lord God Almighty, accept my spirit in peace and send the angel of your peace and your glory that he may teach and guide me toward God. Do not prohibit my ascent from the prince of darkness! Do not shame me before your angels and accept me among your chosed ones, for thou art blessed unto ages of ages." At this point the "stonehearted" torturer jumped on Filipp and suffocated him with a pillow. Upon leaving the cell, he told the prior and the guards that Filipp had died because of their negligence — as a result of extraordinary fumes in the cell. In Maliuta's presence a grave was dug behind the altar of the church and there the martyr was buried.

The *Life* of Filipp ends with God's vengeance upon Filipp's persecutors. Punishment first befell Archbishop Pimen. We have already had occasion to mention the slaughter and massacre of Novgorod. The Tsar spared Pimen's life. Having profaned Pimen in his chambers, the Tsar then exiled him to the Venevskii Monastery. This exile, separated by a few days from the Saint's martyrdom, was not connected with it, at least externally. But the *Life* testifies to the Tsar's later repentance. Ivan became convinced that "he was made to act against the Saint because of cunning" and he subjected all the slanderers to "*disfavor*" [*opala*]. The hegumen of the Solovetskii Monastery, Paisii, was incarcerated on the island of Valaam. Ten other Solovetskii monks were sent to various monasteries. Filofei, the bishop of Riazan', was deposed. Filipp's cruel guard, Stepan Kobylin, was tonsured a monk and sent to the Spaso-Kamennyi Monastery at Lake Kubenskoe.

Basmanov, the *oprichnik* who took off Filipp's vestments in the Cathedral of the Assumption, had already perished. Accused of a plot in favor of Prince Vladimir Andreevich, Basmanov, if we are to believe Kurbskii,

was killed by his own son upon the command of the Tsar
in 1569. Other notorious *oprichniki* laid down their heads
on the executioner's block in the 1570's when, after
the Tatar burning of Moscow, there occurred a sudden
change in Ivan the Terrible's internal policy (after 1572).
The Saint's actual killer was fated to be saved from the
executioner's block. He died in Livonia during a siege
on one of the fortresses in 1572.

Perhaps the cruelest punishment fell on the Tsar.
He saw the collapse of all the great things with which
he had commenced his reign. Defeated by Stefan Batorii,
the Tsar had to give up Livonia, his most precious political
dream. Russia, ravaged and exhausted by the *oprichnina*,
was powerless to continue the war. Within the country
Ivan the Terrible was confronted with a general decrease
in population and a state of impoverishment. And Ivan,
by murdering his own eldest son and also Prince Vladimir
Andreevich, prepared the end of the dynasty. Tormented
by fruitless repentance and by attacks of savage cruelty
and voluptuousness, it seemed as though Ivan was tasting
hell while still alive.

But there was still another guilty party and its
punishment was equally severe. The entire Russian people
were not only Tsar Ivan's victims but also his accomplices.
One ancient historian of this era of discord saw an overall
national guilt in the "mindless silence" before the Tsar.
But the pandering to evil did not end with silence. The
overall demoralization was a consequence of the reign
of the *oprichnina*. People built up their own fortunes
and well-being by becoming rich from the expropriated
properties of those *"disfavored"* and those executed. They
became wealthy through false denunciations. The ad-
vantages of the *oprichnina* service were tempting not
only for rogues but also for representatives of the old
gentry and even for princes (Viazemskii). Even mon-

asteries cooperated with the *oprichnina* in exchange for material well-being. We have seen bishops among the intriguers in the St. Filipp affair. These were individual crimes. Nevertheless, the entire Russian Church and the whole Russian land share responsibility for the council of bishops which condemned Metropolitan Filipp. During those troubled times, the whole land bore the guilt.

In historical events it is extremely rare to ascertain a causal connection which also has a moral significance. It would be nearsighted to look at history as a judicial and also as an infallible process. But sometimes the moral evaluation of events coincides with, or approaches, the pragmatic. Then, an immersion in history gives a moral cleansing similar to the action of tragedy.

There is no doubt about the connection between the *oprichnina* and the troubled times. The discord was a national revolution which responded to the revolution of Ivan the Terrible. The economic and moral shakiness of the people at the time of Ivan the Terrible's death was such that perceptive foreigners such as Fletcher predicted the coming shock.

Something else was obvious from the point of view of Russian religious consciousness. In a theocratical monarchy as ancient Rus' was — or at least attempted to be — the Tsar's sin fell on all the people and demanded national expiation.

But the theocratical character of the Muscovite Tsardom places one very important question before us. Does the Orthodox Tsar who kills a hierarch stand on the same ground with him? In other words, was the murder of Metropolitan Filipp the personal sin of Ivan the Terrible or did it emanate from his idea of power, an idea which was incompatible with Filipp's idea? We must clarify the basic religio-social conflict which stood behind the clash of these historical persons. If St. Filipp had fallen victim to a madman blinded by passion, his martyr's "feat" would not, of course, lose its lofty moral significance. But it becomes increasingly valuable to us if we discern the Church's warning voice, a voice directed against the theocratic idea of the Orthodox kingdom.

CHAPTER SIX

THE ORTHODOX KINGDOM

We have seen that in the persons of the Tsar and the Metropolitan the conflict between Church and State was coming to a crisis long before the time of Ivan the Terrible. Together with the growth of the autocracy of the Grand Princes of Moscow, the hierarchical power of the Metropolitans of all Rus' decreased. Tsar Ivan Vasil'evich only sharpened a tragic contradiction which he was not the first to create. The Tsar spilled the blood of the hierarch and in so doing he shook the very foundation of the *theocratic kingdom*.

Tsar Ivan was not only a "bloody man" but also a learned bibliophile and a brilliant writer who was able to defend himself with the pen. Ivan's need for self-justification was perhaps greater than his impulses toward repentance. From his early childhood years Ivan began to ponder the "divine" character of his power. He was the first of the Moscow princes who, in adolescence, placed the Tsar's crown on his own head and consciously accepted the legacy of those born "in the imperial robes." When Kurbskii's letter stung him later, Ivan took to the pen and in a passionate polemical rebuke he presented his entire theory of his God-established rule. Ivan the Terrible was not, of course, the first in Moscow to discuss the nature of autocracy. But no one expressed his ideas so completely and so acutely. Ivan the Terrible's

political philosophy is not free of contradiction. The
voice of passion too often mutes the voice of reason.
But his shocking and courageous paradoxes are valuable.
They reveal the tendencies of a whole epoch.

Concerning the idea of the divine origin of royal
rule, Ivan wrote: "I was born to rule by the grace of
God." This divine origin coincides with the historical
right of succession. Ivan the Terrible sees the beginning
of "autocracy" in Rus' with St. Vladimir and he sees
its distant roots not only in Constantine's empire but
also in that of Augustus. Ivan the Terrible refuses to
distinguish his rule from that of God. The well-known
apostolic text about subjection to rulers receives the
following interpretation from Ivan: "to oppose a ruler
is to oppose God. And whoever opposes God is an a-
postate, for such an opposition is a bitter transgression."
That is why when Kurbskii betrayed Ivan, he actually
rebelled against God — in the opinion of Ivan.

By its very nature this power of rule cannot have
limitation. "How can an autocrat rule if he does not do
so by himself?" In other countries "of godless people"
it is a different matter: in such countries citizens and
slaves command the sovereign. "But from the beginning
Russian autocracy ruled supreme over its realm; the
magnates and boyars did not rule." In his polemic with
Kurbskii, Ivan the Terrible naturally exaggerated the anti-
boyar and anti-aristocratic aspect of autocracy. According
to Ivan's theory of history, the Byzantine Greek State
perished because of the dominance of the magnates —
because of the "eparchs and the councils." But there is
another aspect to Ivan's theory of history which is more
interesting to us: Ivan the Terrible's idea of autocracy
is also directed against the clergy; more precisely, it is
directed against the clergy's interference in the affairs
of State. This original anti-clericalism of the Tsar was

nourished by bitter memories from his youth. He could not forget how Sil'vestr and the boyar council attempted to decrease his power: "the intention was that I be sovereign in name but co-reign with the priest." He talks about these times with irritation. Or does the "illumination of piety" mean that the kingdom must be in the hands of an ignorant priest?"

It is "ludicrous" to "obey a priest." But again Ivan the Terrible's attitude is based upon his theory of history: every kingdom is destroyed "when it is ruled by priests." Priests destroyed the Byzantine "Greek State and now the Greeks are subservient to the Turks." The destruction of Byzantium is not blamed on the eparchs but on the priests who limited the Emperor's power. For this reason the classic example in the East of an Orthodox theocracy, the very model of Russian theocracy — Byzantium — is not actually a justifiable model in the eyes of the Tsar. Ivan sought corroboration of his anti-clerical idea in the Bible as well. When God led Israel out of Egypt, God did not place a priest or several commoners as the ruler or rulers of the people. God entrusted rule "only to Moses, like a Tsar." Under Moses the priesthood was represented by Aaron. Moses was forbidden to perform priestly functions and Aaron was prohibited from assuming that authority over the people which belonged to Moses. But when Aaron temporarily assumed this authority over the people, the result was that "he led them away from God." The very same thing happened during the days of the priest Eli who "took unto himself both the sacerdotal and lay power." He and his sons died a vicious death and all Israel was defeated before the days of King David. "Do you see how it is not good for the clergy . . . to rule over that which belongs to the Tsar?"

When one reads Ivan the Terrible's distinction

between Moses and Aaron — it may be thought that he was an advocate of the separation of power: the spiritual realm belonging to the clergy, the worldly to the Tsar. But this would undermine the very foundation of theocracy. Such an idea, in any case, is quite foreign to Ivan the Terrible. He acknowledges himself to be God's guardian of faith and piety. "I zealously endeavor to exhort people to the truth and the light so that they come to know the one true God who is glorified in the Trinity, and that they may come to acknowledge the sovereign given to them by God." To the degree that the Tsar's power is dogmatized — rising to the height of the very mysterious life of the Godhood — so also does the Tsar himself appear here as the apostle of dogmas. It is because of Ivan's self-consciousness as the "apostle of dogmas" that he defended Orthodoxy in debates on faith with the heterodox Possevino and Rokita. It is because he took this role seriously that he sent wrathful messages to the Kirillov Monastery about the breakdown of discipline and wrote to Archbishop Gurii of Kazan' about "the flock given to you by God and by us." The parody of monastic life in the *oprichnina* was somehow connected with the Tsar's Church consciousness. He claimed absolute power in the State and Church — except for that which was strictly sacramental — and simultaneously rejected any right of the Church to participate in affairs of State. Herein lies the first peculiarity of his idea of the Orthodox kingdom.

Although Ivan rejects the right of the Church to interfere in matters of State, does he acknowledge that the Church has a right of moral and religious judgment over the Tsar? Does the Tsar, as the son of the Church, have to listen to the voice of the Church? Ivan the Terrible is silent on this topic, but all the evidence leads us to think that he did not want to have intermediaries

between him and God. "You usurp God's right to judge. . .
and you pass sentence even before the day of God's
judgment with an evil and capricious method," he writes
to Kurbskii. He then connects this also with the past
actions of Sil'vestr and Aleksei (Adashev), both of whom
also brought forth accusations. Ivan the Terrible deliberately avoids the question of the Church's right over
him to "edify," restricting himself to the proud pronouncement: "Who has placed a judge and ruler over us?" This
conforms perfectly with his command to St. Filipp in
the Cathedral of the Assumption: "Be silent, but bless
us according to our desire. . ." ". . . Until now, Russian
rulers have not been curbed by anyone." The only lim-
itations on the Tsars' all-powerful rule resided in Orthodoxy — and here only in the narrow sense of matters
related to faith. Only a Tsar's apostasy from the faith
could free the people from their obedience to him. "All
Holy Scripture declares that children should not oppose
their fathers and slaves should not resist their masters,
except in matters of faith."

Ivan the Terrible does not ignore the possibility
of degradation and sinning on the part of a Tsar. But this
in no way frightens him. He boldly points this out to
Kurbskii, using the examples of saints: "many among
them were the fallen and the rebellious." This comparison
was so much to his taste that he developed it in other
details: "And just as they once suffered from demons,
so I have suffered from you." That Ivan's idea of theocracy allowed him to equate himself with saints meant
that he did not recognize any judgment over him on earth.
Herein lies the second personal characteristic of his idea of
theocracy.

The third aspect of his theocratic idea concerned
itself with the methods and problems of imperial service
and purpose. Ivan the Terrible's interpretation of imperial

power included a moral conception: "[The purpose was] to set people on the true path . . . so they desist from internecine strife and unruly life that are so debilitating to the realm." "A Tsar should be calculating, sometimes humble and sometimes wrathful; he should show mercy and humility to the poor, but anger and suffering to those committing evil." But, characteristically, the word "truth" does not enter his mind when he defines imperial purpose and service. His goal is not so much a moral one as it is an educational-police goal — promotion of the good, restraint of the wicked. And the negative goal — education through fear — completely overshadows the positive. Ivan the Terrible is a pessimist in his evaluation of human nature. The recognition of the natural freedom ("self-will") of man is, for Ivan, equal to a return to circumcision. For Ivan, all citizens — without any exception — are slaves, even though the word "slave" [*"rab"*] does not here slip from his tongue — whether he is speaking of the boyars, or the "council" or the priest Sil'vestr. The patriarchal relationship of the Tsar to the people as children, as "wards of the State," gives way to the severe rule of a slave master over his slaves.

Ivan the Terrible keenly and skillfully proves the necessity of the State's punitive and compulsory rule, its distinction from clerical rule, the necessity for the ruler to take the rigorous demands of life into consideration — with what he calls "the current realities of life." But this practical wisdom of government is extraordinarily one-sided. "The imperial rule of a Tsar demands fear, prohibition, restraint and final injunctions because of the mindlessness of malicious and cunning men." He finds these lessons in Holy Scripture and in history. " The apostle commands us "to save with fear" . . . "And you will find that during the time of the pious Tsars there was much of the most horrifying suffering." With an almost demon-like vigilance, Ivan the Terrible points out specific examples of this "horrifying suffering" as the crimes of saintly rulers. "Recall the times of Constantine the Great who, for the sake of the empire, killed his own son? And how much blood did Feodor Rostislavich, our forefather, spill in Smolensk on Easter Day? And yet they are considered to be saints." Even King David impresses him because David "displayed his power and anger even against the feeble."

Within certain limits, this severity of the Tsar's rule is justified if not by service to the good then by the overcoming of evil. But even this thin line is frequently overstepped (as in the example of Constantine), for power takes the place of truth and "ruling" takes on a self-contained pagan character. The "good" become those "seeking to do good" and this "good" is, of course, defined by the Tsar, and those seeking this "good" become the Tsar's "men." "Those who seek good we grace with all kinds of grants, but if they go over to the opposition, then they will be executed according to their guilt." The word "slave" ["*rab*"], which now constantly slips from his tongue, does not go unscathed. It is not used in the Biblical-patriarchal sense but rather in the patrimonial-autocratic meaning, as a substitute for the common usage of "*kholop*." Here the moral relationship ends, giving way to cruel judicial fact. "We are free to favor your slaves and you are also free to execute them." The motive of the master's whim is beyond inquiry. The Christian theocratic idea breaks down and sinks (just as did Ivan the Terrible's governmental reform) in the petty, tyranical habit of an appanage "*oprichnina*" court.

And finally, the last point connected with this is the insensitive secularization within the very core of this idea. Ivan's ideal of power was a pagan, Augustus, under whom the Empire was not yet divided. In Ivan's eyes

Augustus overshadows the Orthodox Byzantine Tsars, and from Augustus, through the legendary *Prus*, he traces his own Riurik kin. In Ivan's contemporary "godless" West and in the Islamic East, Ivan the Terrible looks for lessons in tyranny and easily finds them in the Renaissance era and in the commencing age of absolutism. "You will see how evil works for the wicked in other countries: things are not like here in such countries!. . . There they do not like traitors. They execute them and thereby strengthen themselves."

It is in vain that M. A. D'iakonov, the researcher of Ivan the Terrible's political ideas, claimed that Ivan's opinions "were formed along already existing ideas and that he did not add anything new to the theories at hand." It is true that these ideas are rooted in traditionally Russo-Byzantine Orthodox soil. But Ivan reduces them to the absurd, shaping them into an un-Orthodox and non-Christian form. St. Filipp's ideal of power, which embodied the best traditions of the Russian Church, resisted this perversion of the Russian theocratic idea.

We lament the fact St. Filipp, unlike his persecutor, did not leave us a written work on that ideal of Christ's truth in an Orthodox government for which St. Filipp gave his life. The words of the *Life*, placed upon his lips several decades after his martyr's death, cannot pretend to be original. They do show, however, how the clerical world of the next generation, under the immediate impact of Metropolitan Filipp's "feat," viewed this ideal of rule.

Let us now quote Filipp's words which he spoke in the Cathedral when he had just received St. Peter's Metropolitan's staff from the Tsar:

O devout Tsar, receptacle of God for holy faith. Since you have been the recipient of great benefit, you must then give to Him. God asks charity and good works from us, not just good talk. You have been placed over people because of the loftiness of your wordly kingdom. Be gentle to those who need your help, remembering the power which is above you. Open your ears to the suffering poor and you will turn God's ear to your requests, for the way in which you treat your minions will be how your Sovereign will treat you. Just as a helmsman always keeps vigil, so also must the Tsar's many-sighted mind keep firmly to the rules of good law so as not to dirty the ship of life in the waters of falsehood. Accept those who wish to give you good advice but not those who solicit only favors, for their motive is truly gain whereas the others' motive is the well-being of authority alone. The crown of piety adorns the Tsar more than any earthly glory. It is glorious to display one's power to enemies and one's humanity to those who are submissive. And, in defeating enemies by force of arms, it is glorious to be conquered by one's own unarmed love. Not to forbid the sinful is a sin, for though one may be living lawfully, if one associates with the lawless then he is condemned by God as an accomplice in evil deeds. Stand up for the Orthodox faith firmly and unshakeably. Shake off rotten heretical doctrines so that what our apostles have taught us and what our holy fathers have handed down to us may be preserved. This is how you should reason and how you should lead people who are subordinate to you toward that truth. Nothing in the Tsar's care should be considered higher and more pleasing to God than this.

It is clearly seen that the hierarch does not here limit the Tsar's theocratic power. Just as Ivan the Terrible, Filipp too sees in the Tsar the receptacle of faith, the vessel of a special grace. And he recognizes that the Tsar possesses a certain authority in matters related to faith. But the stress is completely different. The higher the grace, the higher the responsibility. The Tsar is not above truth but is himself subordinate to "good and proper law" — the moral and religious, of course. He is invested with power against enemies (Ivan the Terrible likes to speak not of power but of "fear" and "wrath"). But the first admonition to the Tsar concerns meekness and compassion. The exhortation to have good advisers is specifically concerned with the question of the *oprichnina* and the break with the boyars, although, of course, it is linked with the ideal of truth. Here too, as we shall see, the voice of the Church's past supports Filipp.

In his accusatory conversations with the Tsar, Filipp had occasion more than once to stress the things which separated them. "Maintain the law given to you by God. . . You have been placed by God to judge the Lord's people in truth, not to take upon yourself the image of a torturer. . . Do not divide your realm . . . and unify your people, for God is present only where there is the spirit of oneness and the spirit of sincere love. . . Forgive, and you shall be forgiven . . . Do not put your trust in any kind of justice which is not from God . . . and do not embrace those who are not from God." The truth which the hierarch teaches is not only one of right and justice, but also one of love. The commandment of forgiveness obviously can refer only to the guilty — in Ivan the Terrible's terminology, to the wicked. Instead of wrath, the Tsar must show the face of love even to the wicked. Between the Tsar and the Metropolitan there is a conflict in the very understanding of the problems of government.

The Metropolitan also rejects decisively the Tsar's alleged lack of subjugation to the Church's punitive voice. That is the whole idea of his confession. He speaks of it with tremendous power. "Our silence places a sin on your soul and causes national death." The Tsar, having rejected the accusations, demanded he conform to his opinion. In reply St. Filipp exclaimed: ."Then, O Sovereign, our faith will be in vain as will also be the very Incarnation of God . . . If I maintain silence in matters of truth, then I cannot retain episcopal rank."

In Filipp's words, transmitted to us through his *Life*, there is no special teaching concerning the clergy's right over secular power. But if we are not to speak of power but rather of influence, or the power of the word, the cleric's sword, then Filipp's "feat" is itself a witness to his belief in the indivisibility of the kingdom of truth. In government, as in the Church, the same truth of Christ is manifested and he, the bishop who "cannot maintain silence in matters of truth," is placed as the guardian over it.

Thus, the three basic points of Ivan the Terrible's original idea are condemned by St. Filipp as sin, falsehood and theocratical heresy. It now remains to prove that St. Filipp's point of view was not as "original" as was the Tsar's idea, that Filipp's position represented the positive tradition of the Russian Church.

Here we come up against the following difficulty. The scholars of ancient Russian religious and political ideas distinguish several interpretations of the conception of theocracy, interpretations found among various Russian saints and spiritual writers. These shades of interpretation can be reduced to several points of view — the primacy of the Church, the primacy of the State, and the harmony of Church and State. The era of Ivan III and Vasilii III, a time when the appanage system was liquidated while autocracy was strengthened, is especially rich in the development of political ideas. In what traditions and among which authors are we to seek the answers?

This difficulty partially dissipates when we approach the era of Ivan the Terrible, an era which created a series of secular publicists who left tradition far behind. But we shall not seek the voice of the Russian Church in them, nor in Kurbskii, nor in Ivan Peresvetov. The authentic voice of the Russian Church does not resound too loudly but it is distinctly heard from the lips of Metropolitan Makarii who left the stamp of his personality on a whole era through the decrees of the *Stoglav Council*. One gains the impression that the struggle of opinions troubling the preceding generation receded. Victory fell to Iosif of Volotsk and his disciples, the standard bearers of Muscovite autocracy. Makarii himself can be considered a disciple of Iosif. But the sharp formulations of the beginning of the age softened. Now it was possible to speak of a Church "canon" or "rule" which was even vested somehow in a liturgical form. The more radical founders of the doctrine were St. Iosif and Metropolitan Daniil. We must leave aside the works reflecting individual opinion — the pro-boyar *Conversations of the Miracle Workers of Valaam* [*Beseda Valaamskikh chudotvortsev*] or the Catholic *Short Address* [*Slovo kratko*] , otherwise entitled *On the Freedom of the Church* [*O svobode tserkvi*] .

It is quite probable that Metropolitan Makarii was the compiler of the Tsar's coronation ceremony in 1547 and also the inspirer of the *Stoglav Council*. One idea stands out in these documents, an idea also found in the epistles of Metropolitan Makarii — the idea of "symphony," that is, the harmony of powers of the Tsar and the Church. This idea of "symphony" is usually

ascribed to Maksim the Greek, although his views in
general often differ in many aspects from those of the
Russians. Nowhere and in nothing is there a limitation
on the power of the Tsar in matters related to the Church,
for which he is the "watchful guardian" ["*opasnyi khra-
nitel'* "], the "perfecter and maintainer" ["*ispravitel' i
utverditel'* "] of the Christian faith. The reverse side of
the Tsar's ecclesiastical power is the Church's participation
in the affairs of government. The same Ivan the Terrible
who rejected this Church right in his letters to Kurbskii
allowed the council to discuss and confirm the regulatory
chapters of the *zemstvo's* self-government . . . "so that
each affair and all customs in our kingdom be structured
according to the Lord . . . And we call on your episcopal
council for action and advice and we wish to seek your
counsel about God." The Russian clerics had no taste
for worldly affairs. They did not consider participation
in the affairs of government to be their right but rather
sometimes their duty, a view expressed in one of Metropolitan Makarii's political letters to Lithuania. Commencing his letter with "we are Churchmen and this is not
our affair" (i.e. the Tsar's diplomatic affairs), the Metropolitan continued: "And we, as Christian priests, remind
the crowned autocrat that he should maintain peace and
tranquility with his border neighbors."

The Church's participation in worldly affairs is
natural because the world, too, is subject to Christ's
truth. In the sermon to the Tsar given during the coronation ceremony Metropolitan Makarii urges him to "rule
the people in truth," to love "truth, charity, and justice,"
and "to fear the heavenly judgment." The idea of mercy
or even of counsel is inseparably linked to this idea of
truth: "favor your boyars and magnates and preserve the
fatherland through them. And, according to your rank
and office, be kind, friendly and accessible to all your

princes, your serving princes [*kniazhata*], to your lesser gentry [*deti boiarskie*] and to your entire God-loving army." The ideal in Maksim the Greek is fully in accord with this: "The Tsar is a living and visible image of the Heavenly Tsar, but the Heavenly Tsar is the source and substance of beneficence, the complete truth, all-merciful and generous to all." To that same Maksim the Greek belongs the successful formula of "truth and beneficial law" by which the Tsar must structure his kingdom. In contrast to Ivan the Terrible, Maksim the Greek ascribes an inner logic to autocracy, considering "a true autocrat" only a Tsar "who orders the life of his subjects according to truth and beneficial law." The Tsar's law, of course, demands punishment for the guilty and the *Stoglav* reminds us of the "Tsar's wrath," but within the perspective of an ideal kingdom this threat is decisively in the background.

It was the duty of priests, especially of bishops, to guide the Tsar on the right path of service; it was their duty to rebuke the Tsar just as they could rebuke any lay person, especially since they had taken a vow to do so even if threatened with death. Metropolitan Makarii recognized this no less clearly than did St. Filipp: "In being consecrated . . . we vowed before all the people to preserve our laws and destinies . . . and . . . not to be silent before the Tsar in matters of truth. And if the Tsar or his magnates attempt to force us to speak other than the holy laws, then we shall not listen to them and we must not obey even if death is threatened." So Makarii writes in his reply to Ivan the Terrible's suggestion about the limitation of the Church's ownership of land. In taking such a position, Makarii appeared to be in opposition to the Tsar's unfair wish. And the Tsar, in his speech before the council, reminds the hierarchs of their vow, imploring them to oppose any violation of "holy laws." "Do not

be silent about this. I will be attentive. Prohibit me without fear and may my soul and all those under our power
live." In impressing the Tsar with his duty, the clergy
not only lightened their conscience; they also expected
that their words would not be in vain. In the coronation
ceremony the Metropolitan demands that the Tsar "render
his spiritual obedience in the name of the Holy Spirit to
all the clergy — for the sake of humility." The question
of the limits of this obedience of the Tsar was not raised
but it is unlikely that it was "prescribed" by just a circle
of clerics.

The priest Sil'vestr's precept to Shuiskii — which
concerned not so much the Metropolitan's relationship
to the Tsar as the relationship of the clergy to the lay
world in general — expounded the duties of the clergy
in this way: "to intercede, to entreat, and to exhort the
worldly rulers in all possible ways on behalf of the victorious, the guilty, and the offended; and if they do not
obey, they are to be rebuked and interdicted."

It is common to consider St. Iosif of Volotsk as
the most consistent champion of Muscovite autocracy.
Truly, the highest conception of the divine rule of the
Tsar belongs to Iosif. One may conventionally speak of
the subordination of the Church to the State in Iosif's
teachings. His definition is well-known: "By nature the
Tsar is similar to all men; but as ruler he is similar to
God above." But the burden of responsibility corresponds
to the loftiness of the rule. "Much torture awaits the
powerful and the strong." The Church cannot leave the
Tsar with the burden of sins before the face of God, "for
God punishes the whole land for the Tsar's sins." That
is why even obedience to Tsars has limits and why service
to them is distinguished from service to God. "It is befit-
ting for subjects to bow and serve the Tsar physically but
not spiritually; they may render unto the Tsar his imperial

honor but are not to venerate him as divine." How is one
to act if a Tsar becomes a sinner and torturer and demands
obedience? Iosif boldly raises this question in the seventh
chapter of the *Enlightener* [*Prosvetitel'*] and then answers
it:

> If there is a Tsar who rules over men, and who is
> ruled by evil passions and sins, by greed and wrath,
> cunning and falsehood, pride and anger, and worst
> of all by lack of faith, and one who abuses, such a
> Tsar is not a servant of God but of the devil and is
> not a Tsar but a torturer. You should not listen to
> any Tsar or Prince who leads you to impiety and
> cunning, even though torture or death threatens
> you. Witness the prophets, apostles, and all the
> martyrs, for they were killed by impious rulers
> because they did not submit to the commands of
> such rulers.

Thus Iosif, who created the notion of the Tsar's God-like
power, also constructed the teaching about the Tsar-
tyrant and of the legal struggle against such a tyrant. A
comparison of Iosif's teaching with that of the Western
supporters of monarchy in the sixteenth century would
be interesting.

The features or characteristics of the tyrant St.
Iosif portrays and the legal means of disobeying such a
Tsar are remarkable. For Ivan the Terrible, as we have
seen, there is only one basis for the people to disobey a
Tsar — if the Tsar errs in matters of faith, then the people
may disobey. For Iosif it is the whole boundless sphere
of moral crimes: "impiety and cunning." Metropolitan
Daniil, who was true to his teacher, and despite his practical opportunism, also placed moral limits on the Tsar's
arbitrariness: "Princes and sovereigns have power over

bodies but not over the soul . . . Therefore, if they order us to murder or commit other inordinate acts which can damage the soul, it is not proper to obey even though the body be tortured unto death. God has made the soul free and self-determining, to do good or evil."

If Daniil could write this way, it may be safely assumed that all the hierarchs of the Russian Church had to think in the same manner. But because of human weakness they rarely had the courage to follow this dangerous path — "unto death." St. Filipp did what St. Iosif and Makarii taught. It was precisely he who in the sacrifice of his life expressed the idea of Orthodox theocracy. He was neither an innovator subverting the traditions of autocracy nor a reactionary admirer of appanage-boyar antiquity, though his personal moral tie with that system may have cultivated his sensitivity and independence. He perished not for a dying mode of life but for a living idea — Christ's truth which held the whole Russian theocratic kingdom together. The Russian realm cruelly trampled this idea in practice but could not reject it without denying itself. The century in which St. Filipp lived shook this idea incessantly. The century kept moving further away from the ideal of "symphony," from the harmonious relationship between Church and State. The martyr's death could have been a sacrifice of atonement that saved the country, if the country had accepted it and participated in it. This did not happen. And St. Filipp's blood overfilled the cup of the sins of the Russian land which was already full to the brim. The impending collapse became spiritually and morally inevitable. No matter what the social causes of the catastrophe were, a society cannot live by daily killing the idea of its very existence. An Orthodox kingdom without truth is a corpse from which the soul has departed. "Where the corpse is, the vultures will gather."

CHAPTER SEVEN

THE GLORIFICATION OF ST. FILIPP

If the murder of Metropolitan Filipp was the sin of the Tsar and the whole Russian land, then his glorification must be linked to an act of national penitence. Long before Russia's "Time of Troubles" [*Smutnoe vremia*] penitence had begun. First to be penitent were the monks of the Solovetskii Monastery who had betrayed their spiritual father. And the son of the Tsar who had killed Filipp evidenced penitence.

In 1590, twenty-one years after St. Filipp's death, Iakov, the hegumen of Solovetskii Monastery, came to Tsar Fedor Ivanovich with a request from all the brethren. He said:

> Grant us our citizen Filipp who was exiled from his throne by the calumny of his disciple and who was buried in a place which was foreign to him. From youth he labored together with the elders of the monastery and now we are bound by duty to rectify the harm which his disciples caused him. Your imperial permission will again grant us that blessing of which we have been deprived.

The Tsar gave the hegumen a message to convey to the bishop of Tver' whose name was Zakharii. When the martyr's grave was dug up in the court of the Ostroch

157

Monastery, it was discovered that his relics were unde-
cayed. The people of Tver' came to venerate the saint
who was leaving their city. With reverence hegumen
Iakov transferred the sacred relics, now entrusted to him,
by means of waterways to the northern monastery.

The brethren greeted their holy one triumphantly
and buried him under the parvis of the Church of Saints
Zosima and Savvatii in the very place St. Filipp had picked
for himself while he was still alive. Soon healings and
miracles began to occur.

The beneficiary of the first miracle performed by
St. Filipp was a carpenter named Vasilii, "a newcomer
from the eastern land" who was preparing logs for the
renovation of the church. He had been crushed by a
falling tree in the forest and lay a cripple for three years.
He prayed that St. Filipp would heal him. Then, on
Christmas day, when those nearest him had gone to
church and had left him alone, he saw in a dream that
he was standing in church at vespers and in front of
him was St. Filipp in episcopal vestments with a censer
in his hand and completely encompassed by light. The
saint approached the invalid and said: "Arise, Vasilii,"
and, having raised him by the hand, added: "Be healed
in the name of the Lord and walk!" Upon awakening,
Vasilii discovered that he was in fact healed and went
to church by himself to thank the saint.

Soon after this the enfeebled monk, Isaiia, who
was in charge of the kitchen, was healed at Filipp's grave.
The third to be healed was Ivan, a smith from the shore
of the Varzuga River. Ill for a long time, Ivan had once
seen in a dream a saintly man in the vestments of a hierarch and the man asked him: "What is your illness?" When
the sick man pointed to his stomach, the man in the
vision blessed him and said: "Do you not know me? I am
the Metropolitan from Solovki." Having recovered, Ivan

went to Solovki and related what had happened to him.
That is how the fame of St. Filipp's miracles spread. The
inhabitants of the coastal region flocked to the island to
venerate him. His *Life* was compiled during these years
by a monk unknown to us. The author evidently was not
a witness to Filipp's years spent in Solovki. About himself
he writes: "From these people and from others I have
heard authentic stories about him." He writes, however,
the following about Metropolitan Filipp's activity in
Moscow: "I have seen this myself rather than hearing it
from others." At some time, probably in the beginning
of the seventeenth century, another *Life* of Filipp was
compiled in Solovki, one which portrayed the Solovetskii
hegumen's practical work and the suffering of his incarceration in more detail. The latter *Life* was based to some
extent on the testimony of the guard, Kobylin, later to
become elder Simeon "who was secluded on Solovki."

Under Patriarch Ioasaf I, who was himself a Solovetskii monk, the liturgical service commemorating St.
Filipp was entered into the printed *Minei* of 1636 and
the day of his commemoration was celebrated on the
twenty-third of December. But only ten years later were
the saint's relics opened and transferred to the Cathedral
of the Transfiguration. The report of the celebration —
a report by Il'ia, the Solovetskii hegumen, to Patriarch
Ioasaf — has been preserved.

Five years later this same Il'ia was elevated to the
rank of archimandrite and from this time on he was the
prior of the Solovetskii Monastery. A year thereafter —
in 1652 — another transfer of St. Filipp's relics took
place — this time to Moscow. This event occurred in the
last year of the life of Patriarch Iosif, a weak man who
did not have much influence on Tsar Aleksei Mikhailovich.
Thus, it is natural to view Nikon, the Tsar's favorite and,
at that time, the Metropolitan of Novgorod, as the in-

itiator of this unusual celebration. A monk of the Aizerskii hermitage in Solovki, Nikon, like Patriarch Ioasaf, had a particular zeal for St. Filipp and personally sought Filipp's glorification. But the way the Moscow celebrations of 1652 were planned reveals that Nikon had his own religio-national idea. It was determined by an act of a council to transfer the remains of three Moscow hierarchs to the Cathedral of the Assumption for burial: those of Metropolitan Filipp, Patriarch Iov (who was exiled to Starits by the "False" Dimitrii and died there), and Patriarch Germogen (who was tortured to death by the Poles in the Chudov Monastery). All three hierarchs were zealots of the national, popular cause and all fell victim to tyrannical rule. By returning the hierarchs to the house of the Mother of God, to their patron church, it can be assumed that Moscow and, above all, the Tsar, were repenting for the sins of their forefathers. It was an act which reconciled the land to its sacred heroes. Varlaam, the Metropolitan of Rostov, along with the boyar Saltykov and a large retinue, were sent to Starits for Iov's coffin. Nikon took the most honored assignment upon himself. He was not only to transfer the remains of a metropolitan but also the relics of a glorified miracle-worker. He was accompanied by Prince Khovanskii and many gentry and servitors. The boyar retinue underscores the popular, national character of the celebration.

On March eleventh, after prayer in the Cathedral of the Assumption, the Tsar dismissed both embassies — one to go to near-by Starits, the other to distant Solovki. The remains of Iov were greeted in Moscow as early as the fifth of April. The Patriarch wept and told the Tsar: "See, sovereign, how good it is to stand up for the truth. There is glory after death." In a few days Iosif, already advanced in years, died.

Because the ice on the White Sea thawed quite late,

Nikon arrived in Solovki only on the third of June. On
the road Nikon had received a letter from the Tsar in-
forming him that the Patriarch had died and that the Tsar
had nominated him — Nikon — as successor. The Tsar
ended the letter by wishing Nikon a peaceful and safe
journey. At sea Nikon's ships were dispersed by a storm.
One vessel perished without a trace; others broke against
the cliffs. Finally, surviving "the great passions of the
sea," they reached the wharf. After a prayer of thanks-
giving, Nikon placed two messages on the saint's shrine —
one from the Tsar, the other from the Patriarch. After
three days of fasting and prayer, Nikon loudly read the
Tsar's "message to Filipp" during the liturgy. Although
this address was patterned after Emperor Theodosius'
address to the deceased John Chrysostom — even the
supplication to forgive the sin of the father is the same —
it is nevertheless remarkable as a monument to the living
faith and pure soul of the meek and quietest [*tishaishii*]
Tsar.

> To the imitator of Christ, the heavenly dweller,
> incarnate angel beyond nature, our refined and
> wise spiritual teacher, our pastor and intercessor,
> great lord, father of fathers, right reverend Filipp,
> Metropolitan of Moscow and all Rus', by the will
> of the Almighty, Tsar Aleksei, your child, greets
> you in the name of the saints. Nothing would
> relieve the sorrow of my soul so much as to have
> you, holy lord, in our city of Moscow, preserved
> by God, in the great and famous cathedral and
> apostolic church . . . Secondly, I pray to you and
> desire that you come here, if the sin of our great-
> grandfather, our Tsar and Grand Prince Ivan, per-
> mits, a sin which victimized you because of ir-
> rational jealousy and uncontrollable wrath. And

if your indignation is also directed at us as accomplices in his evil deed, it is written: the harshness of parents sours the children. Even though I am innocent of your vexation, my great-grandfather's coffin convicts me and leads me to grief. . . For this reason, I bow in my imperial dignity for him who has sinned against you that you forgive him by your coming here . . . I pray to you for this and bow my anointed head and submit the honor of my kingdom to your venerable relics. I petition you with all my power that you may come here and forgive the vain abuse you received. Would that he had become penitent at that time for what was done. For the sake of his penitence and for our forgiveness, come to us, holy one. You have accomplished the word of the Gospel, for you have suffered for it and because of you there will be no division in the realm. And there is no controversy about the commandments of God. And there is the grace of God in your flock and it is in abundance in our kingdom because of the prayers of the saints. And there is no division now in your flock. . . now we unanimously request and beseech you to come in peace to your own place and your own people will accept you with love. O holy one, saintly sovereign Filipp, our pastor! We beseech you — do not deny our sinful supplication. Come to us in peace. Tsar Aleksei wishes to behold you and to venerate your holy relics.

According to Nikon, the entire church wept at the reading of this letter and he could barely read because of his own weeping. The archimandrite requested that a small piece of the relics remain in the monastery. Nikon writes: "And when I your *bogomolets*, began to take a

part of St. Filipp's holy relics, I smelled much sweet
fragrance and many others were able to smell the fragrance." Covering the tomb of the saint [*raka*] with a
shroud provided by the Tsar, they carried the holy relics
to the boat. "On the way many people fainted from
weeping and tears . . . they lay about on both sides of
the road like fools [*obiurodevshie*], some overcome by
happiness, some by sorrow. . . " Having gone some five
versts from the monastery, they stayed at Zaiatskii Island
for two days and waited for a change in the weather.
Twenty-four hours thereafter they safely entered the
mouth of the Onega.

Nikon kept the Tsar informed about the progress
of the journey by writing detailed letters. On the twentieth
of June they sailed up to Kargopol'. From there they
moved overland to the Kirillov Monastery and, on the
twenty-fifth of June, sailing on the Sheksne, they reached
the village of Rybnoe (Rybinska) on the Volga. From
here overland travel began again on the great northern
road — through Pereiaslavl', the Holy Trinity Monastery,
and on toward Moscow. On the stopovers everywhere the
relics were taken into churches and services were held
with large crowds of people. The last stopping place was
in the village of Vozdvizhenskoe, some six versts from
the lavra where Nikon awaited the Tsar's orders. He did
not venture to take the priceless relics into the wooden
church of the village "because of the multitudes and the
poor arrangement of the candles." Instead, he waited
with them "under a moveable shelter — in a tent."

On the ninth of July Moscow greeted its great
saint. A religious procession left the Cathedral of the
Assumption; it was led by Varlaam, Metropolitan of
Rostov. Behind him came the Tsar in a gold caftan with
an Indian staff of ivory, in a crown studded with jewels
and pearls. Huge crowds filled the streets of the Naprud-

naia settlement [*sloboda*] where the Tsar met the holy relics of the saint near the chapel. A cross made from oak was erected on this spot and the name "Gate of the Cross" was bestowed upon it.

Here the general happiness was darkened by a sad event. The elder Varlaam could not endure the fatigue and the heat of the July day. Having sat down in a chair, he suddenly died right at the saint's relics. But the Tsar was already in a hurry to take the holy burden upon his own shoulders. The deceased metropolitan was carried behind St. Filipp. The subsequent procession and the miracles which occurred on that day were described by Aleksei Mikhailovich himself in an enthusiastic and e-motional letter to Prince N. I. Odoevskii:

> God has given us a great sovereign, a great sun. Just as the relics of the most radiant John Chrysos-tom were returned to the ancient Emperor Theo-dosius, so also God has granted us a healer, a new Peter, a second Paul the preacher, and a second Chrysostom, the splendid and most radiant sun. We have been granted the return of the relics of the miracle-worker, Filipp, Metropolitan of Moscow and all Rus'. And we — I, the Grand Sovereign; our *Bogomolets* Nikon, Metropolitan of Novgorod and Velikolutsk and presently by the grace of God, Patriarch of Moscow and all Russia; and the council, the boyars, and all Orthodox Christians (even in-fants) — we greeted the relics of Filipp at the Naprudnaia settlement, and took the relics upon our heads with great honor. As we were taking them, a miracle occurred — a raving and dumb woman immediately became well and began to speak. When we came to the elevated area [*lobnoe mesto*] in (Red Square), another miracle took place.

A girl was healed in the presence of the Lithuanian envoys who were standing by the area and everyone shed tears. The pastor who was unjustly persecuted returns again and ascends his throne. And when we brought them to the square across from the Granovitaia, here again a miracle occurred. A blind man was healed and, just as in the days of Christ, people cried — have mercy on us, Son of David! And there were so many people along the way from the Naprudnaia settlement to our apostolic Cathedral that there was no room for an apple to fall and there was a constant moaning from the crying and the wailing of the people. And Filipp's relics remained in the middle of the church for ten days and during those ten days the bells rang without cease. Those days were joyous ones, just like those of Holy Week. At least two or three people a day were healed. On some days as many as five, six or seven were healed. And when Patriarch Nikon was consecrated, the radiant miracle-worker Filipp healed two on that day. And even now a river of miracles flows. Stefan Veliaminov's wife was healed. She had requested that the prayer for the dying be read and she had already become oblivious. The saint came to her and said: "Ask to be taken to my coffin" (she was blind, had been deaf for eight years, and had also had a head injury for all those years). And when she was brought there, she immediately began to see and hear, and she arose and went away in health. And he heals not only those who have been sick for eight years but also those who have been ill for as long as twenty or thirty years. He heals bleeding women, the insane, and those ill with all kinds of ailments. And who would not wonder at this, glorify this, and weep to look upon the exile who has again returned and been received with great honor? Who would not marvel when his radiance was brought to the apostolic Cathedral and placed on his former throne? Where are the slanderers, the tempters, those with eyes blinded by bribery, and those wishing to take power at the expense of the persecuted? . . .

And the Tsar concludes with a prayerful appeal to the heavenly powers in which he reveals how well he understands Filipp's martyrdom and its meaning for the Russian land.

> O blessed commandments of Christ! O blessed unhypocritical truth! O blessed is he, and thrice blessed, who carried out Christ's commandments and suffered for them from his own people. Truly, one can choose no better than to be glad and joyous in truth, to suffer for it, and to reason with God's people about truth. And we, the Grand Sovereign, daily ask the Creator that the Lord God would grant us, the Grand Sovereign, and you, the boyars, the ability to mutually judge this people in truth, all equally; for it is written: God's judgment does not dwell in falsehood . . . and we have concern for all Christian souls, and it is our duty to stand strong and pillar-like in faith and in truth, and to suffer unto death unto ages of ages.

In this letter the Tsar's exultant confidence in the already present triumph of truth and the total expiation of old sins is remarkable. The same mood is apparent in his "prayerful message" to St. Filipp. "God's grace prevails in our kingdom and there is truly no division in your flock." If there was a moment of equality in the stormy history of Russian Tsardom, if there was a "symphony" in the realization of the idea of theocracy, then it was precisely in the middle of the seventeenth century. Tsar Aleksei Mikhailovich was perhaps the only one worthy of wearing the sacred crown. Humble, devout, almost a saint — he astounds us with the strength of his faith, the childlike purity of his heart, and his thirst for truth. And what happened? How history mocked his sacred hopes! Only a few years separate the exultant words of his letter from a new, severe "division." Once again the Church and the Tsardom would clash in a mutually agonizing struggle. This time it was not to be the Tsar's fault. Within a few years the cruel division passed through the whole body of the Russian Church, splitting it in the name of different understandings of that very "faith and truth" which Tsar Aleksei Mikhailovich — until his dying day — asked be defended. Again social convulsions, Razin's revolt, and the rebellion of the infantry regiments [strel' tsy] shake the national body. And then emerges the gigantic specter of the Emperor who gave the death blow to Holy Rus' and, it seemed, overthrew all the foundations on which the ancient and sacred Tsardom was established. Theocracy in Russia ended in derangement and with it came the collapse of national culture. The splendid flowering of the cult threw a shroud of sacredness over the falsehood about which the Russian land screamed in a thousand voices. This falsehood was not seen by the pious Tsar just as the "terrible" Tsar, who wrote the following, did not see it: "God's churches shine with all kinds of decorations and good things . . . but we have no martyrs for the faith at this time." Thus wrote the Tsar who gave the Russian people the greatest of her martyrs — a martyr for truth. But the ancient Russian Church, as represented by its best sons and clergy,

never separated faith from truth and truth from mercy.
And the last Moscow Patriarch stood before the new,
stern Tsar with an icon of the Mother of God in his hands,
a silent soliciter on the morning of the executions of the
strel'tsy . . .

The Church remembers the service of the faithful
pastor, prayerfully appealing to the holy martyr: "To
the successor of the rulers of the highest throne, pillar
of faith and champion of truth, to St. Filipp, who gave
his life for his flock."

APPENDIX

APPENDIX I

HISTORICAL EVALUATIONS OF THE OPRICHNINA

The evaluation of the *oprichnina* we have presented may seem out-dated and "un-scholarly" to the reader who is familiar with research on the subject. True, it appears that our approach is more similar to Karamzin's approach than to Vipper's [Wipper]. Some works by Russian historians have frequently rehabilitated the *oprichnina* and, with it, the rule of Ivan the Terrible — sometimes to the point of apotheosis. For this reason the author, who is also a specialist in Russian history, feels obligated to defend his point of view.

For the Christian, of course, the complexity of this historical problem is significantly simplified. St. Filipp was not a politician but rather a defender of "truth" in a Christian State. One may conditionally allow the governmental necessity of the *opirchnina* revolution and the severe measures in the struggles with the boyar opposition. It does not matter. There remains the general character of immorality, contempt for human justice, the tyrannical "bloodthirsty" cruelty that is not justified by any governmental considerations. For historians of the "social school" these are minor details, "excesses" which do not lessen their admiration of the system. For the Christian who believes in evaluating things from a spiritual perspective, the main criterion in judging a political figure is that person's moral quality. That is why

171

we, in evaluating Ivan the Terrible and the *oprichnina*, tend to be in accord with the conservative historians of the "old" school — such as Karamzin and Ilovaiskii — even though we evaluate the meaning of the processes of Russian history differently.

In this case, however, do we take cognizance of the tragic contradiction between the religious and the national-political evaluation? Perhaps good fruit grew from the evil seeds sown by Ivan the Terrible? Perhaps his revolution strengthened the Russian State and guaranteed it years of power and glory? This contradiction between the heavenly and the pragmatic and earthly constitutes one of the most powerful temptations for a person trying to interpret history from a religious perspective. Let us not expand this problem to the realm of historical theodicy. In the given case it is enough to point out that in this most important knot of Russian history there is no such hopeless contradiction.

In the few pages of an "appendix" this can be shown in only one way: by indicating the conclusions which have been reached by truly objective historical scholarship and by looking at the bases upon which the "scholarly" *apologia* of the *oprichnina* rests.

Here we encounter one remarkable fact. A careful study of the very scant materials on the history of the *oprichnina's* regime has given us nothing which can really allow such an institution to be justified. At the basis of those favorable evaluations are preconceptions, the various afflictions of a "positive" scholarly mind. To uncover these preconceptions is the duty of any objective historian, especially if one is interested in religious history.

The question of the *oprichnina* is irrevocably connected with the general evaluation of Ivan the Terrible and his place in Russian history.

S. M. Solov'ev initiated the reaction against the

Karamzin school and against the Slavophiles (K. Aksakov
and Iu. Samarin). This reaction was founded upon and
directed against the personal, psychological and moral
approach to Ivan the Terrible which left his *era* without
specific attention and which degenerated into a dilet-
tantish subjectivism. Solov'ev intended to present "objective" history. But his objectivism is nurtured in the
Hegelian school. This means that he is a prisoner of the
idea of the "wisdom of reality" and views the historical
"process" optimistically, as the triumph of a loftier
principle. As we know, for Solov'ev this loftier principle
is State authority in a struggle with the vestiges of the
patrimonial system. The sixteenth century is the era
of the government's final defeat of the patrimonial traditions with appanage principalities and boyar rights.
It is claimed that in the struggle with the boyars Ivan
the Terrible is the carrier of a higher principle. It is this
which determines the evaluation of some historians.
Such a position goes beyond the scope of obvious ob-
jectivity. The most unjust judgment occurs, for the accused — that is, the defeated — are not even heard. This
occurs because the historian constructs the image of
Ivan's rule exclusively on the basis of official — that is,
governmental — sources. The absence of documents or
reports of the judicial process, for example, force Solov'ev
to exclude the information of the victims of the terror
about which many contemporaries speak. The ultimate
impression left by such historians is almost comely and
politically decent. Of course, Solov'ev does not close his
eyes to the negative consequences of the *oprichnina*.
"As the creation of enmity, the *oprichnina* understandably
could not have a good and moderating influence." There
is mention of the destructive separation or "departure of
the head of government from governing," his rejecting
to rule through his "instruments of power." There is

mention also of the inescapable abuses of the "favorites." But still the reader familiar with Karamzin feels as though he is in a totally different world, one which is bloodless and deprived of life's colors. And the sources utilized are actually scantier than those used by Karamzin because Solov'ev rejected the sources written by "foreigners." A large part of Solov'ev's sixth volume treats the events of foreign affairs but this history is not depicted in connection with the domestic. The reasons for defeat in the Livonian War are not clear. Several observations about the ugly excesses of the *oprichnina* do not help at all in understanding the process and inner workings of the *oprichnina*. It may be said that faith in the wisdom of the *oprichnina* is demanded of the reader, despite its clearly catastrophic origin.

Other contemporaries of Solov'ev, especially the representatives of that same "historico-juridical" school, drove the idealization of Ivan the Terrible to the point of absurdity. K. D. Kavelin considered Ivan the Terrible to be a "great" precursor of Peter the Great; Ivan, it is claimed, was destroyed by a "dull, mindless" environment. The analogy to Peter was also drawn by Bestuzhev-Riumin who considered both sovereigns to be men of "the same character, with the same goals, and with almost the same means for achieving them." For the Westernizers of the nineteenth century, the analogy to Peter the Great was already sufficient justification for respecting Ivan the Terrible. One thing was strangely forgotten: that Peter created an empire whereas Ivan almost destroyed the realm. Unfortunately it seems that the main standard of evaluation for most historians is historical success.

Thus, for the historians of this orientation, the *apologia* of Ivan the Terrible flowed from their preconceived optimistic conception of the "historical process" and also from their exaggerated evaluation of the

State.

In a rather strange way this positive evaluation of Ivan the Terrible also filtered through to certain circles of the Russian intelligentsia, to those circles where the State was viewed in almost anarchistic terms. The positive element which many perceived in Ivan the Terrible was the "democratic" principle. Ivan crushed the patrimonial aristocracy and placed the positions of power in the hands of the lower gentry. In the eyes of many this was a merit which atoned for everything. No one asked himself the following question: what did Russia really gain for itself from the forced destruction of the old, cultured, freedom-loving ruling class, a class which was historically interconnected with the town communities [*miry*] and with ancient, national traditions? And what did Russia acquire through the revolutionary incursion of a mass of rogues, Tatars, Cossacks and runaway criminals into the ranks of the ruling class?

V. O. Kliuchevskii combined the spirit of democratic sympathies with an understanding of the governmental tasks of the Muscovite realm. But his "Great-Russian" perception caught the contradiction between the triumphant enthusiasm of an Orthodox Tsar and the petty capriciousness of a tyrant. Kliuchevskii treats Ivan the Terrible ironically. He does not judge Ivan's moral character but rather his renowned mind. Kliuchevskii does not want to bring forth those bloody specters evoked by Karamzin. He evaluates Ivan the Terrible as a ruler and comes to the conclusion that his inconsistency, discrepancies, his dissoluteness — which lay at the basis of his character — had a destructive political influence. This verdict he also extends to the *oprichnina*.

Perhaps Kliuchevskii treated the *oprichnina* a bit simplistically. He saw the *oprichnina* as no more than a "corps of gendarmes" ready for political battle. It was

Professor S. F. Platonov who clarified the "social" meaning of the *oprichnina*.

In his work entitled *Essays on the History of the 'Time of Troubles'*, S. F. Platonov uncovered the agrarian content of the *oprichnina* reform: the transferring of servitors from one district to another destroyed the ancient ties between the boyars and the population, especially in the central regions of the government. The *oprichnina* was initially depicted as an attempt to create a new military-servitor class with the goal of building upon the foundation of the *oprichnina* a new, powerful statehood forever freed from the appanage-princely traditions. Platonov's work was continued by his "school" and the continuation relied on new documentary materials and studied the organization or structure of "ruling" in the *oprichnina* or, as it became, in the "courtly" part of the government. One result of this research was that the calculated and systematic character of the *oprichnina* was discovered, whereas previously one saw only a convulsive tyrannical reaction. Also monographic studies of other aspects of administration in the era of Ivan the Terrible tended to elevate the political capabilities of this sovereign. From this, however, it is a long way to a positive appraisal of this system. The head of the Petersburg historical school himself did not and could not reach such conclusions, for he linked the study of the *oprichnina* with the genesis of the great disturbance — the "Time of Troubles." Only the revolutionary era brought forth a series of apologists of the *oprichnina* and at the same time there was a tendency which worked toward the apotheosis of Ivan the Terrible.

The latter attempt was undertaken by R. Iu. Vipper [Wipper]. In his brilliant book which is rich in ideas — *Ivan the Terrible* (Moscow, 1922) — Vipper, treating Russian themes for the first time, depicted Ivan within the framework of the European and Asiatic sixteenth century. For the first time a link was established between Moscow's foreign and domestic policy. The author deserves full credit for calling attention to this international setting. But in the study of Russian affairs Vipper does not include new materials nor does he employ a new method. His book is not a study but rather a panegyric. He is full of passion and behind his apologetic exterior he conceals a hatred which was nourished then by the contemporary events through which Vipper lived. He wrote his book under the agonizing impression of the destruction of the Russian Empire. Hence, in elevating Ivan the Terrible, Vipper unleashes his anger at the liberal and humanistic persons of the preceding century, persons who were unsympathetic toward the idea of "stern" rule. Like Machiavelli, Vipper, in his patriotic pain, seeks a tyrant and consoles himself retrospectively, resting in the Moscow of Ivan the Terrible rather than in the Moscow of 1917. Vipper was always a materialist. In history he saw only the blind and senseless play of forces. He exhibited a phenomenal blindness to the realities of spiritual life. But the contemplation of the power of the triumphant force (Rome) was a source of historical inspiration for him. Actually Vipper does not descend to an admiration of Ivan the Terrible's terror. He is content, however, with his justification of it. The *oprichnina*, in his estimation, was an attempt to expand the government's military forces in the extraordinarily difficult circumstances of war. The destruction of Novgorod forced a "correction of the shaken military position" etc. . . The *oprichnina* reflects the striving of "democracy" in the sixteenth century. The democratic council of 1566, in its break with pragmatism and common sense, is linked with the establishment of the *oprichnina* in 1565. Vipper interprets the conversion of the *oprichnina* into a "court" in 1572 as the expansion of the system under the influence of the "betrayal of Novgorod" (Vipper's quotation marks) and the Crimean invasion. Vipper does not surmise (and this was clarified with the publication of Staden's memoirs) that the reform of the *oprichnina* in 1572 was, in actuality, a reaction in which the chief officials of the *oprichnina* perished. He does not surmise that the burning of Moscow by the Crimean Khan revealed to the government the unreliability of the *oprichnina* forces and the importance of having a "landed army." For Vipper, understandably, the final catastrophe of the Livonian War remains incomprehensible. "The fate of Ivan IV is a real tragedy of the conqueror who was ruined in a game with stakes that were too high because he threw all his possessions on the scales of fortune and, together with the loss of colonial spoils, deeply shattered the bases of the old Empire." Vipper does not notice that this is the most severe judgment one can pass on a political statesman. In unusually captivating fashion, Vipper depicted the might of the Muscovite State created by Ivan III. Now it turns out that the ingenious Ivan IV (who is compared to Peter the Great) lost the inheritance of his ancestors in a game of chance.

Vipper's book drew a responsive chord from Russian historians (A. Presniakov's review in *Annals*, No. 2) mainly because of the novelty of the ideas and the historical analogies. But the explanation for its great success also lies in the spirit of the time. In various essays on Russian history, the historian M. N. Pokrovskii, one of the leaders of Bolshevism, presented an apology of Ivan the Terrible. Historical materialsim and a spirit opposed to morality makes him akin to Vipper. Even if we allow for the differences of political views, nevertheless these historians still belong to the same "school." The justification of tyrants is one of Pokrovskii's favorite historical themes.

It is nourished by a common Marxist hatred, a hatred of all forms of aristocracy and of the very idea of freedom. Pokrovskii interpreted Ivan the Terrible as the leader of the democratic revolution and justified such an interpretation on the same grounds as he justified the "democrat" Paul I and the Decembrists.

The essay by I. I. Polosin, written as an introduction to Staden's memoirs, is a most curious mixture of the two styles of thought — Vipper's and Pokrovskii's. Against the background of a broad picture of the international relations of Muscovite Rus', Polosin depicts the *oprichnina* as a "real social revolution" without which "Ivan the Terrible's brilliant accomplishments would be unthinkable." The strenthening of the position of the small landowners was considered the *fact* of this revolution. It seems that the term "social revolution" frees the author from proving its political value. Somewhat surprisingly, on the next page (page 41) we read: "The subsequent intensification of the social revolution threatened the existence of the State." The study of Staden was not in vain for the author: "Tsar Ivan was a nervous politician, but a sensitive one. He himself became the head of the reaction," which turned out to be inevitable after "the ruthless, stern measures of the revolutionary years." Why did the Tsar's agrarian measures inevitably achieve a "ruthless, stern" character? There is no answer unless we turn to the psychological influence of the two periods of Leninism on this author — the era of "war communism" and the era of "NEP."

S. F. Platonov's brief study, *Ivan the Terrible* (Petrograd, 1923), came out a year after Vipper's book. Although it is only a "brochure," it summarizes the results of almost a half-century's work by this highly regarded specialist. Every word in this study is thought out and weighed. Without solemnicizing, the author defends his interpretation of the old moralists and the more recent apologists. Calmly and confidently, the master Platonov puts all things in their place.

S. F. Platonov retains his high opinion of Tsar Ivan's political talents. For him Ivan the Terrible is a "great figure." The introductory chapter can even give the impression that the author has contemplated still another apology for the tyrant. However, the more the reader goes into the depth of the history of the reign, the more the familiar image of Ivan looms before us. Ivan the Terrible appears the same way as he was depicted by the conservative historians of the nineteenth century. The author does not want to "cite details of the persecutions and executions" but in his careful characterization of the Tsar he acknowledges "abnormalities." He also acknowledges "the feeling of fear before non-existent dangers," "elements of a persecution-complex," "sadism, i. e. the combination of cruelty and depravity," and even the lack of courage. But we are primarily interested in the evaluation of the *oprichnina*.

In speaking of the "domestic disorder of Muscovite life" that led to defeat in the war with Batorii, S. F. Platonov indicates that there were dual reasons for such disorder. "Some cause for disorder lay with the so-called *oprichnina* of Ivan the Terrible and its consequences. Another cause was rooted in a spontaneous phenomenon — the working mass of the Muscovite population activated themselves; they became mobile and, in abandoning its permanent way of life, started to move away from the center toward the outlying districts of the State."

In this way, the *oprichnina*, beginning as a means of assistance in a difficult war (Vipper, Polosin), becomes in fact the cause of defeat. Having drawn a broad picture of the agrarian class (without stopping at the "excesses"), the author turns to its consequences:

> First of all, the revision of the princely land holdings turned into an overall mobilization of the land; it was compulsory, troublesome, and hence disorderly (at least in the *oprichnina*) . . . All layers of the population which fell subject to the activity of the *oprichnina* suffered agricultural loss and, willingly or unwillingly, were forced out of their permanent settlement into a mobile, if not a wandering, one. The stability of the population, which was attained by the State, was lost and in this case it was the State's own fault.

> Secondly . . . Ivan the Terrible thought it necessary to link this operation with political terror, with executions and with the disfavor [*opala*] of individuals and entire families, with the destruction of princely estates, and with the annihilation of entire districts and cities. With the development of the *oprichnina*, the government entered into a state of domestic war for which, however, there was no reason. The Tsar persecuted his enemies who did not fight him.

> The result of this mindless and totally unnecessary terror was the complete dissolution of the country's domestic relations . . .

> There was bitterness in other layers of the population, just as there was among the boyars. The *oprichnina* and terror were despicable to all except to those who tied their worldly success to them. They set the whole population against the cruel rule and, at the same time, they introduced dis-

sension within the ranks of society. According to the accurate observation of the Englishman G. Fletcher, who was in Moscow soon after Ivan the Terrible's death, the base politics and the barbarous acts so aroused general discontent and irreconcilable hatred that this evidently had to end in a way no other than by general revolt. This observation, made before the "Time of Troubles," was fully justified by subsequent Muscovite events.

Thus the conclusions of Platonov's scholarship coincide with the unanimous opinion of contemporaries — both Russian and foreign — and with this conclusion the feat of Metropolitan Filipp is justified not only spiritually but also from a political point of view.

APPENDIX II

ST. FILIPP'S
LETTERS TO SOLOVKI

LETTER I

The humble blessing of Filipp, Metropolitan of All Russia, to the elders Iov and Paisii, to the steward [kelar'] and the treasurer [kaznachei], to the priests and to all the brethren of Christ. How is God favoring you? Are you all prospering in salvation? Here in Moscow God has given good health to Ivan Vasil'evich, Tsar and Grand Prince of 'All Russia, to the Tsarina and Grand Princess Mariia, and to his children Prince Ivan and Prince Fedor, and to Prince Vladimir Andreevich, the princes and boyars, and all Orthodox Christians — everyone is presently blessed with well-being through the prayers of the Mother of God, the great miracle-workers Peter, Aleksei and Iona, and of all the saints. And God's will has come to pass. The Tsar and Grand Prince, and the Tsar's sons — the royal princes — and the archbishops and bishops, and the princes and boyars have forced me, the unworthy one, upon this great throne of All Russia.

And I bless you that you might live in love of Christ and look after your immortal souls and that you might preserve the monastic rule. I have not mentioned the matter of hegumen to the Tsar and will not without your advice. When you need a hegumen, let me know of

this in due time and send me a message about the one
whom you would wish to have as hegumen and the one
whom God will bless.

And I bless you and petition you. For the sake of
God, pray to the Lord God and to his ever-virgin Mother,
and pray to the great miracle-workers Zosima and Savvatii
and to all the saints — pray both in common and in private — for the Orthodox Tsar and Sovereign, Grand Prince
Ivan Vasil'evich of All Russia. And pray for the Tsarina,
Grand Princess Mariia, and for their children Prince Ivan
and Prince Feodor. Pray also for Prince Vladimir Andreevich and for the Christ-loving army, for all Orthodox
Christians and for me, a sinner. And for the sake of God,
may you all — elder Iona, the priests, and all the brethren
in Christ — forgive me, a sinner, for transgressions great
and small. . . I am doubtlessly guilty in all things before
all of you [*Pered vsemi esmi vami vo vsem vinovat bez
razuzhdeniia*] . God will forgive all of you.

I have sent to all the brethren a pound of pepper,
some cloves [*grivenka*] and some saffron for fish soup
[*ukha*] . Otherwise, prosper in Christ. Peace to you.

LETTER IV

The blessing of Right Reverend Filipp, Metropolitan of All Russia, to the most honorable, great cloister of the Holy Transfiguration of the Lord, our God and Saviour, Jesus Christ, and of the holy saints and great miracle-workers, Zosima and Savvatii, to the Solovetskii Monastery and its spiritual father, son and co-worker of our humility, hegumen Paisii, and the priests, the elder Iona, and to the steward [kelar'] and the treasurer [kaznachei], and to all the brethren in Christ.

How is God favoring you? Are you all prospering in salvation? And I, Filipp, by God's grace, by the Sovereign's royal well-being, and by your holy prayers, am alive in body. And may the Lord forgive you for the fish which you sent me — the twenty salted fish and the nine fresh uncut fish. The fresh fish were small in size — there were few of the medium size and twelve fish were rotten. The half barrel of herrings and the one and a half pails of pond herrings were also in bad shape. In this may God not bless you, for you have given me great sorrow. I had ordered you, hegumen Paisii and the elders — and I had sent letters — that you send me nothing to feast on, and no fish. But you do not listen to me. And you have given me great grief both in Moscow and in the monastery. You have caused me to complain . . . May God not count this as a sin.

I have sent to you through Stepan Makhilev two large silver plates for the *antidor* [na doru] which can be used for both large and small altar bread. The plates cost me close to thirty rubles. I also sent a larger silver serving spoon and a large copper basin with handles for blessing water. You should receive them and then let me know about it. And I have sent you ten rubles in coin with the servant, Seliuga, to be used for the pond that is behind the court. You should clean it well, for the pond will be great and laudable and to abandon it because of human litter would be a sin before God. All former labor would be lost. The dam is ready as well. It only needs to be cleaned. I have ordered the elder Misail and Seliuga the servant to do this. They will make it ready for you and it will bring praise to the monastery. You will then begin to put in fish, for fish will keep well there and will multiply. When I left for Moscow, I had left three pipes and a pole. They should be taken and placed into the Zaiatskie waters. For the sake of God, let it be done. I ordered Seliuga to do it and he will complete it as God gives him grace. You should favor him for God's sake and for my sake. I ask you on behalf of your love for me to keep me informed about this. And if you do not favor Seliuga, you shall not make Paisii hegumen . . . And I ordered Misail and Seliuga to hire some people and to feed them from their own bread. Should you not favor them and allow them to do so, you should let me know. I gave Gerasim the money he spent coming to Moscow and bringing the fish — I gave him three less than thirty *altyny*. In Moscow they ate and drank in my quarters until they set out to return.

I sent to you through Gerasim and Seliuga eight rubles worth of *kvas*, three rubles of alms for the brethren, a half *altyn* each for the two hundred brethren, and for the some three hundred children one and a half rubles. And you, hegumen Paisii, for the sake of God, prepare a feast for the brethren, the servants and the children. Serve *kvas*. And at the feast you should remind the brethren to pray for the good Tsar and Sovereign, Grand Prince Ivan Vasil'evich of All Russia, for the Tsarina and Grand

Princess Mariia, for the good children, Prince Ivan and Prince Feodor, for the Christ-fearing army, for all Orthodox Christians, and for me, a sinner. Remember all of us in your holy prayers. I bless you and humbly ask much of you. Let God's grace and the grace of the Holy Mother of God and the great miracle-workers, and their prayers, be with you. May God's grace and our humble blessing remain with you unto ages. Amen.

Written in Moscow in the year of 7076 (1568) on the thirtieth of January.

And I bless you and humbly beseech hegumen Paisii and all the brethren to live in love, for the sake of God.

Glossary of Terms

AKATHIST HYMN– The Akathist ["not sitting"] Hymn was, according to tradition, composed by Patriarch Sergius of Constantinople (610-638). When the city was besieged by the Persians, the people placed the city under the protection of the Holy Virgin. When the enemies dispersed and the siege was lifted, the people interpreted it as a miracle. Patriarch Sergius then composed the famous hymn. To show honor and respect, the people in Hagia Sophia stood throughout the entire service (hence the name Akathist Hymn). The Akathist Hymn or hymns are sung on Friday night during Lent. The Akathist is divided into twenty-four sections, each section beginning with a letter of the Greek alphabet. According to the Typikon, there is only one Friday when it *must* be sung; that is, the matins of Holy Saturday during the 5th week in Lent.

ALTYN (pl. *altyny*)– An altyn (which was derived from the Tatar word for six–alty) was a monetary unit equivalent to approximately six *den'gi* or three copecks.

BIRICH (pl. *birchi*)– A *birich* was a policeman whose function was to announce government orders to the people. Hence a *birich* was like a herald or towncrier.

BLACK CLERGY [*Chernoe dukhovenstvo*] – "Black Clergy" was the term used to refer to the monastic clergy. All other clergy were referred to as "White Clergy" [*Beloe dukhovenstvo*].

BOGOMOLETS– This was a term which expressed the spiritual relationship between the Metropolitan of Moscow (or other bishops) and the Sovereign of All Russia: A *Bogomolets* was one who prayed on behalf of the Sovereign. The term also can refer to (1) any religious person; (2) a pilgrim; or (3) anyone who prays for someone else.

BOBYL' (pl. *bobyli*)— The *bobyli* were the lowest class within the peasantry. Most of the *bobyli* possessed no property at all; others possessed small cottages while a few held small areas of arable land. One connotation was that a *bobyl'* had no family connections.

BOYAR [*boiarin*] — The *boyars*, also known as the *kniazhie muzhi* [the prince's men] were the top-ranking members of a prince's *druzhina*. The *boyars* became owners of large estates, functioned as the aristocracy, and rendered "service" to their princes.

CHIN— A *chin* in Muscovite Russia referred to a group of men, all of whom belonged to the same profession or class. For example, there was a *voinskii chin* [warrior men] and a *iereiskii chin* [priestly men]. *Chin tsarskii* was the royal insignia. The word became associated with rank.

CENSER— A censer is a metal vessel in which incense is burned. It is suspended by four or five chains and has a moveable cover. The censer is handled easily by the priest or deacon who raise it by gently swinging it and hence produce incense in the church.

CHET' or *CHETVERT'*— A *chet'* was either "one-quarter" or, as in sixteenth century Russia, a term used for dry measurements of grain. A *chetvert'* was the equivalent of one *pud* (36.133 pounds).

CHETII-MINEI (pl.)— The *Chetii-minei* are the monthly readings. In the sixteenth century Metropolitan Makarii of Moscow collected everything then existing in Russia; that is, the lives of saints, sermons, exegetical works on the Bible, selections from the Church Fathers, etc. This material was then put into a monthly reading cycle. The work of Makarii filled twelve large volumes.

CHISLO— The word *chislo* means number. A *chislo* was a census of the population which began under the Mongols for taxation and military purposes.

DACHA— In Old Russia a *dacha* was property given as a grant.

DENGA, DEN'GA (pl. *dengi* or *den'gi*)— Although this Mongolian-derived word today means "money," *den'gi* in Old Russia were specific coins. In the fifteenth and the beginning of the sixteenth century the *den'ga* in Novgorod was the equivalent of two Moscow *den'gi*. In the middle of the 1530's Moscow minted new *den'gi*, the *dengi kopeinye*, which, because they doubled the older Moscow *den'gi* in weight, were equivalent in value to the Novgorodian *den'gi*.

DIAK or *D'IAK* (pl. *d'iaki*)— A *d'iak* was a secretary and as such the *d'iaki* formed the basis of Russian bureaucracy. A *d'iak* could be attached to the boyars, to the chiefs of departments [*prikazy*], or to the *namestniki*.

DESIATSKII (pl. *desiatskie*)— A *desiatok* was the officially recognized unit which was formed by ten households. These ten households then elected a *desiatskii* who functioned as a police official and was in charge of keeping order within the *desiatok*.

DETI BOIARSKIE— The plural term *deti boiarskie* referred to the "lesser gentry" in Muscovite Russia.

DOR— *Dor* was an old term for *"antidor."* *Antidor* (which literally means "instead of the gift") is the small piece of bread which is cut from the altar bread after the necessary pieces have been cut for the Holy Eucharist. The "gift" of the Divine Liturgy is considered Holy Communion. For those who do not receive Holy Communion, the *antidor*, which is blessed, is distributed after the service.

DOVODCHIK— A *dovodchik* was one who dealt with *dovod* [evidence, proof, indictment] and hence was connected with the system of courts and jails. A *dovodchik* was a bailiff, a prosecutor or a constable.

DVOR— The term *dvor* could refer to either a household, a settlement, a yard or a court. Quite often *dvor* referred specifically to those men who "served" a prince militarily. It also referred to all those who "served" a prince.

DVORETS— A *dvorets* was either the palace itself or the central office which managed the land and persons of a palace.

DVORIANIN (pl. *dvoriane*)— A *dvorianin* was a courtier. In Muscovite Russia the *dvoriane* held landed estates and were under obligation to serve in the military. The *dvoriane* also held administrative positions in the government. The *dvoriane moskovskie* consisted of approximately one thousand of the "best" provincial *dvoriane* who were given large estates near Moscow in exchange for serving as a Tsar's guard.

EIS POLLA ETI, DESPOTA— *Eis polla eti, Despota* is the refrain sung during liturgical services in the Orthodox Church when a bishop is present. Literally it means: "Unto many years, O Master."

EPARCHY— An *eparchy* is an administrative subdivision of the Greek Orthodox Church; it is a diocese or a bishopric.

GORODOVOI PRIKAZCHIK— A *gorodovoi prikazchik*, according to the *Sudebnik* of 1550, was supposed to verify the arrests made by the local *namestniki* and *volosteli*.

GOST' (pl. *gosti*)— In Muscovite Russia the *gosti* were the wealthiest and the elite of the merchants. The Tsar bestowed the honorary title of *gost'* on these merchants and they helped in the collecting of State taxes.

GOSUDAREVY SIROTY— Whenever a peasant or a poor person addressed the Tsar, such persons referred to themselves as *"tvoii gosudarevy siroty"* ["your Soveriegn's poor or orphans"].

GRIVNA (pl.*grivny*)— A *grivna* in Old Russia was a unit of weight or also a monetary unit. In Muscovite Russia at the time of Ivan the Terrible the *grivna* was equal to approximately twenty *den'gi*.

HERBERSTEIN, BARON SIGISMUND VON– Baron Sigismund
von Herberstein (1486-1566) was born in Vipava, part of present-
day Yugoslavia. Although his native language was German, Herberstein knew Latin and Italian well and had some knowledge of Greek,
French, Russian and Polish. Herberstein studied law at the University of Vienna and in 1514 entered the service of Emperor Maximilian I.

Baron Herberstein visited Muscovite Russia twice: the first visit
was made in 1517 as ambassador of Emperor Maximilian I; the
second visit occurred in 1526 as ambassador of King Ferdinand I.
As a result of his experiences in Russia, Herberstein wrote *Rerum
Moscoviticarum Commentarii*, a work which appeared in many editions and was extremely influential in forming Western views of
Russia.

At least two English editions of *Rerum Moscoviticarum Commentarii* exist: 1) *Commentaries on Muscovite Affairs*, ed. and trans.
by O. P. Backus. University of Kansas Press, 1956; 2) *Description of
Moscow and Muscovy 1557*, ed. B. Picard; trans. J. B. C. Grundy.
Dent, London, 1969.

HETMAN (pl. *hetmany*)– The word *hetman* is derived from the German *Hauptmann* (a "head man" or the "chief man," a "captain"). In
Old Russia a *hetman* was a supreme military commander. Its main
usage in Russian history is in the context of Ukrainian and Cossack
history.

IURODIVYI (pl.)– The *iurodivyi* were "Holy Fools," "Holy Fools
in Christ" or "*bozhie liudi*" ["people of God"]. Although the
emphasis in Russian spirituality was a bit different, the tradition of
the *iurodivyi* can be traced to the Byzantine *salos*. To a certain extent, the *iurodivyi* resemble some of the "primitive prophets" in
ancient Israel whose behavior has been preserved in the books of
Samuel and *Kings*. The *iurodivyi*, however, became a rather specifically Russian spiritual phenomenon.

The "holy fools" warned Russia of impending doom, urged the
people and leaders to become more ascetical, and practiced them-

selves forms of spirituality which some consider "excessive," "self-abasing" or "abnormal." The *iurodivyi* travelled constantly. They played the food because it gave them the possibility to speak the truth in this way.

IZBRANNAIA RADA– The *izbrannaia rada*, usually translated as "Select Council" or "Chosen Council," came into existence during the young years of Ivan the Terrible. This "inner" circle attempted both to protect Ivan and to further the interests of the boyar class. Two central figures in the *izbrannaia rada* were Metropolitan Sil'-vestr and Aleksei Adashev whom Ivan later called respectively a "churlish priest" and a "dog."

KELAR'– A *kelar'* (from the Greek *kellarios*) was a "steward" or a "manager" of the lands and people connected to a monastery.

KHOZHDENIE "POSOLON"– *Khozhdenie "posolon"* literally means "going in the direction of the sun"; i.e. from East to West. The direction of a religious procession became controversial in Old Russia and, later, with the Old Believers, it became a focal point of religious controversy.

KNIAZ'– The word *kniaz'* means prince. A *Velikii kniaz'* was a Grand Prince.

KNIAZHATA– *Kniazhata* was a word which referred to all "serving" princes collectively.

KORMLENIE (pl. *kormleniia*)– From the fourteenth to the sixteenth century local administrators (*namestniki* and *volosteli*) in Russia received no payment from the higher authorities. The position of these administrators was bluntly known as the *kormlenie* or the "feeding" system. Fines went directly into the pockets of the administrators, though the administrators were also paid with foodstuffs. Payment–in either kind or coin–was called *korm*. In 1555-1556 Ivan the Terrible attempted to abolish the *kormlenie* system totally, replacing the *korm* with the *obrok* [tax] which went directly into the Tsar's treasury.

Vestiges of the *kormlenie* were not abolished until the seventeenth century.

KUKOL'– A *kukol'* is the Slavic for a cowl which was a monk's hood or the hooded robe of a monk.

LOBNOE MESTO– The *lobnoe mesto* was the "elevated place" in Moscow from which official proclamations were read.

LUCHSHIE LIUDI– The *luchshie liudi* were the "best people"– both economically and morally. The term was almost synonymous with the *bol'shie liudi*, the *dobrye liudi*, or the *viashchie liudi*.

MIR (pl. *miry*)– A *mir* was usually a peasant community, though other types of *miry* existed: *posadskie miry* [communities formed by towns folk] and *vseuezdnye miry* [communities formed by the entire local population]. Ivan the Terrible's reforms in the 1550's granted the *miry* much self-government.

NAMESTNIK– During the fourteenth through the sixteenth century, a *namestnik* was a local administrator, sometimes a judge. Such local administrators were appointed directly by the Grand Prince or Tsar.

NASTOIATEL'– *Nastoiatel'* was a term which referred to a prior or superior of a monastery or a rector of a church.

NESTIAZHATELI (pl.)– The "*nestiazhateli*" were the "non-possessors." Followers of Nil Sorskii, the "*nestiazhateli*" believed that monasteries should follow the rule of poverty and not only "not possess" but not even try to possess either land or money. (See under "*zavolzhskie startsy*"). The "*nestiazhateli*" became known as the "*zavolzhskie startsy*" ["Trans-Volga elders"] since their monasteries were "across the Volga." In 1525-1526 the "*nestiazhateli*" accused Tsar Vasilii III of divorcing his wife unjustly. Tsar Vasilii III incarcerated most of the "*nestiazhateli*" and closed their monasteries.

OBROK— In Old Russia an *obrok* was a fixed sum of money which was paid either for taxes or for services. Ivan the Terrible, when he granted self-government to local communities, demanded that these communities pay *obrok* to the Sovereign instead of paying, as previously, sums [*kormy*] to the *namestniki* and *volosteli*. The term *obrok* also meant rent, usually the renting of State properties.

OKOL'NICHII (pl. *okol'nichie*)— The word *okol'nichii* is derived from the word *okolo* (meaning "around") and hence referred to those who were "around" or "near" the Grand Prince or Tsar. The *okol'nichie*, courtiers of the Tsar, ranked after the Boyars in the Old Russian aristocratic system.

OPALA (pl. *opaly*)— In Muscovite Russia *opala* was the term which referred to someone's falling out of favor with the Tsar. "*Opala*" was a "right" possessed by the Tsar; it was receiving his official "disgrace or disfavor," sometimes resulting in exile or punishment.

OPASNAIA GRAMOTA— An *opasnaia gramota* was an official document [*gramota*] which promised or assured "safe conduct."

OPLECH'E— The word *oplech'e* (pl.), now obsolete, referred to the "shoulders" of garments.

OPRICHNINA— The word *oprichnina* is related to the word *oprich* which means something "set apart." in 1565 Ivan the Terrible established a state within his State by creating a new state institution known as the *oprichnina*. A special section in Moscow was sent aside for the *oprichnina* headquarters, though the central headquarters were northeast of Moscow in the *Aleksandrovskii* settlement. A reign of terror began. Thousands were slaughtered and Ivan the Terrible seized the estates of many of the boyars, princes and other landowners, giving such estates to his new corps of men [*oprichniki*] in the *oprichnina*. The reign of terror passed after 1572 and Ivan the Terrible disbanded the *oprichnina*. It was meant to serve as a private army, a personal cabinet, and an organ to supervise and watch over the national administration.

PANAGIA– *Panagia* is the Greek word for "All Holy" and one of the titles bestowed upon the Virgin Mary. It is also the name of the small icon of the Virgin which hangs upon the chest of a bishop along with the pectoral cross.

PAPERT'– A *papert'* was a church porch or a *parvis.*

PARVIS– A *parvis* is an enclosed garden or courtyard in front of a church.

PECHAL'NIK– A *pechal'nik* was an intercessor, one who interceded with higher authorities on behalf of someone else. The term referred also to the Metropolitan of Moscow who had the "right" to intercede before the Tsar on behalf of persons or on behalf of the Church.

PECHALOVANIE– *Pechalovanie* was the act of intercession, usually the act of intercession of the Metropolitan of Moscow. *Pechalovanie* had been a recognized right which belonged to the office of the Metropolitan of Moscow. St. Filipp, before his consecration, fought to restore this right of intercession to the office of Metropolitan.

PISTSOVYE KNIGI– *Pistsovye knigi* (pl.) were the census books or cadasters in Muscovite Russia.

POMEST'E (pl. *pomest'ia*)– A *pomest'e* was a *fief*; that is, land given in exchange for military service. In Muscovite Russia there were only two types of land: (1) the *votchiny* belonging to the boyars or monasteries; and (2) all other land which theoretically belonged to the Grand Prince or Tsar, and which the Tsar could grant in exchange for life-long military service–*pomest'e*. One who held a *pomest'e* was a *pomeshchik.*

PORUKA– *Poruka* was a guarantee or a bail.

POSADNIK– A *posadnik* in ancient Kiev was usually a lieutenant appointed by a prince to govern a district or city. The situation in Novgorod was different. Since the Novgorodian *veche* was virtually independent, it was the *veche* which called and dismissed a *posadnik.*

POSTRIZHENETS– A *postrizhenets* is one who is being *tonsured* or one who has taken monastic vows, vows which are symbolized by the act of *tonsuring.*

POSTRIZHENIE– *Postrizhenie* is admission to the monastic life by means of *tonsuring.*

PRAVO– *Pravo* was a law, a right, a norm or regulation. It also carried the meaning of power or procedure connected with a court.

PRIKAZSHCHIK [or *prikazchik* or *prikashchik*] – In Muscovite Russia a *prikazshchik* or *prikazchik* was a government official who administered his district or town by receiving instructions from Moscow. The *Sudebnik* of 1550 states that a *gorodovoi prikazchik* was supposed to verify the arrests made by the local *namestniki* and *volosteli.*

PRISTAV (pl. *pristavy*)– A pristav was a police official.

PUD (pl. *pudy*)– A *pud* was a measure of weight equivalent to about 36.113 English pounds. The term *pud* could also mean a scale on which something was weighed or the payment for weighing something.

PUSHKAR' (pl. *pushkari*)– In Muscovite Russia a *pushkar'* was an "artillery man" or a maker of cannons. The more common meaning was that of an "artillery man." Such a position became hereditary with the *pushkari* living in their own settlements [*slobody*].

RADA (pl. *rady*)– The word *rada* literally meant *"advice."* A *rada* was therefore a council or members of a council.

RAKA (pl. *raki*)– A *raka* is a saint's shrine.

RAZRUB (pl. *razruby*)– In Muscovite Russia the *mir* elected officials called the *rasrubnye tseloval'niki* [sworn appraisers] who then levied taxes. The decision of what tax was paid by whom was the *razrub.*

RIZA– A *riza* was a chasuble or the priestly garment which the Greek

Orthodox refer to as *felon*. It is a long, sleeveless garment which is worn over all other garments. It symbolizes the seamless coat of Christ. A vestry or sacristy in Russian is *riznitsa*.

SAZHEN (pl. *sazheni*)— A *sazhen* was a measure of length which was equivalent to approximately seven feet (or 2.133 meters). Its measurement, however, fluctuated in various local places.

SIROTA (pl. *siroty*)— In old Russia the word *sirota* meant either an orphan or a poor person. The term came to embrace the peasants and the lower class of the city population. When they addressed the Tsar, such people referred to themselves as *"tvoii gosudarevy siroty."*

SLOBODA (pl. *slobody*)— A *sloboda* was a "settlement" or an area embracing the same types of persons. Usually the *slobody* had special tax privileges. There were various types of *slobody* in Old Russia.

SLUZHILYE LIUDI— In Muscovite Russia the *sluzhilye liudi* were those who "served" the government, the State, the Sovereign. The *sluzhilye liudi* had many sub-divisions but the term essentially referred to those who "served" in a military way. Those serving in a "non-military" way were usually referred to as *"prikaznye liudi."*

SMUTNOE VREMIA— The *"Smutnoe vremia"* or, in English, the "Time of Troubles" began after Ivan the Terrible's death in 1584 and continued until 1613 when the Romanov dynasty ascended the Russian throne. The generally accepted historical periodization is 1605—1613, although one could argue that it, psychologically at least, began before or with the death of Ivan the Terrible.

STAROSTA (pl. *starosty*)— The *starosty* were the "elders" or the political leaders who were elected by their respective communities. Also a warden.

STARETS (pl. *startsy*)— In Orthodox monasticism the *starets* or elder (from Greek *geron*— *"elder"*) is a monk recognized as possessing wise spiritual discernment. The *starets*, who could be a lay monk or a hiermonk, functioned as a spiritual guide. Etymologically, the word can refer to any old man.

STOGLAV— The word *stoglav* literally means "one hundred chapters." In 1551 a Russian Church Council adopted a revised manual, took a stand on "correct ritual" and prescribed regulations for a better governing of the behavior of both clergy and laity. The decisions of the Council were in a "Hundred Chapters" and hence the apellation of Stoglav.

STRELETS (pl. *strel'tsy*) — The word *strelets* literally means a "shooter." The *strel'tsy*, though formed earlier, were organized into regiments about 1550 with the purpose of forming a permanent military force. At that time their number was estimated at about twelve thousand. Although a *permanent* military force, the *strel'tsy* were allowed to participate in trade and industry in peacetime. Toward the end of the seventeenth century many *strel'tsy* became *Starovery* [Old Believers]. This, along with political problems, caused riots among the *strel'tsy*. The riot in 1698 led Peter the Great to execute more than one thousand *strel'tsy*.

SUDEBNIK (pl. *Sudebniki*)— The *Sudebnik* was the Code of Law in Muscovite Russia. There were three *Sudebniki*: the first was in 1497; the second in 1550; and a third in 1589. The most important was the second which contained information on all types of regulations and laws in one hundred articles.

SUDEBNYI PRISTAV— A *sudebnyi pristav* was a court bailiff.

SVIATITEL' (pl. *sviatiteli*)— A *sviatitel'* was any of the higher ranking hierarchs of the Church such as a Patriarch, Metropolitan, Archbishop or Bishop.

TIAGLO, TIAGLA or *TIAGLY*— The term apparently entered Muscovite Russia as a result of the Tatar rule and it signified a type of "burden" or "obligation." The term *tiaglo* referred to all obligations — labor and monetary — which the government imposed on "registered" persons. The term also came to refer to the "ability" or "potential" of those imposed to meet their obligations.

TIAGLYE LIUDI– The term referred to those "burdened persons" who were officially registered with the government and under "obligation" to perform some work for and pay taxes to the government.

TIUN (pl. *tiuny*)– A *tiun* was an agent of various ranking officials in Old Russia. In Muscovite Russia a *tiun* could also be a steward, a bailiff or a judge.

TORGOVYE LIUDI– A *torg* in Old Russia was a marketplace or commerce in general; hence *torgovye liudi* were "trading people." The term embraced all those engaged in trade except the wealthiest of traders who were called *gosti*.

TSELOVAL'NIK– In Muscovite Russia a *tseloval'nik* was one who served the central government. When taking the oath to serve the government, the *tseloval'nik* kissed the cross and Holy Scripture. Hence the name: *one who kissed*.

TSREN (pl. *tsreny*)– A *tsren* was an iron pan which aided the evaporation of salt.

TYPIKON– The *Typikon* is one of the most essential liturgical books of the Orthodox Church; it gives the directions for all the services.

TYSIATSKII– The word "*tysiatskii*" literally means a "thousand (men)." The *tysiatskii*, selected by the prince (except in Novgorod where the *veche* was responsible for appointing a *tysiatskii*), was essentially the commander of the military. In Novgorod the *tysiatskii* was the second highest official (the first being the *posadnik*). The last *tysiatskii* in Moscow died in 1374 and the Grand Princes never appointed another one.

UDEL'NYI PORIADOK– This term, which means "the partitioned or divided system," specifically referred to the custom among ancient Russian princes of dividing their property among their children. It then referred to the reality of the property actually possessed by the princes. The term is commonly translated as the "appanage system."

VOEVODA (pl. *voevody*)– Literally a *voevoda* was a commander of warriors [*voi*]. In Muscovite Russia a *voevoda* was either a military commander or, especially later, a governor of a province.

VOTCHINA (pl. *votchiny*)– The word *votchina* (or *otchina*) most clearly resembles the word *patrimony*. The word originally referred to land which was *inherited*; land which was bought was referred to as *kuplia*. Early in the sixteenth century the word *votchina* took on a broader meaning; it came to refer to land owned by either the church or by lay persons. Later still the term became synonymous with the land possessed by a "landowner" until, after Peter the Great, the word declined from the langage; then the term *pomeshchik* signified landlord.

There were various types of *votchiny*: *Kuplenye votchiny* – properties which were *bought*; *Pridanye votchiny* – properties received as a dowry; *Rodovye* (also: *starye*) *votchiny* – properties inherited from ancestors; *Vysluzhennye votchiny* – properties received in exchange for, or as a reward for, service; *Zhalovannye votchiny* – properties given by the Sovereign.

VOTCHINNIK (pl. *votchinniki*)– A *votchinnik* was one who possessed a *votchina*.

VECHE– The *veche*, a word related to the verb *veshchati* [to speak], was a local assembly or a town meeting. In ancient Russia each town or city had its *veche* which all "freemen" could attend.

The most famous *veche* in ancient Russia was perhaps the Novgorodian *veche*. Toward the end of the eleventh century all administrative positions of Novgorod were "elective positions," even the position of archbishop of Novgorod (after 1156). Until Novgorod was defeated by and annexed to Moscow in 1478, the *veche* of Novgorod was the most significant Novgorodian political instrument, its functions combining the executive, the judicial and the legislative powers.

Vechnye d'iaki — were the secretaries of the assembly [*veche*] whose main function was to prepare the documents [*gramoty*] which contained the decisions of the *veche*.

Vechnye gramoty — the documents or "charters" of the *veche*.

VECHNIK — The term *vechnik* referred either to a member of the town assembly [*veche*] or to the bell used to convoke the assembly [*veche*].

VERST— A *verst* was and is a measurement of distance which is 2/3 of a mile.

VOLST' (pl. *volsti*)— Literally the term *volst'* meant power or government (it is related to the modern Russian word *vlast'*). It meant, however, a territory or a district. In Muscovite Russia a *volst'* also referred to peasant communities which formed a *mir*.

VOLOSTEL' (pl. *volosteli*)— From the fourteenth to the sixteenth centuries a *volostel'* was the head administrator of a rural district. The *volosteli* were the rural counterparts of the city *namestniki*. Each *volostel'* was in charge of a *volost'* [a territory, region or district].

VYVOD —The word *vyvod*, which literally means an "exodus" or a "leading out" or a "conclusion," was a condition included in treaties made by the people of Novgorod, a condition which prohibited any "exodus" [*vyvod*] of population from Novgorod.

ZAVESHCHANIE DUKHOVNOE — A *zaveshchanie dukhovnoe* was a last will and testament.

ZAVOLZHSKIE STARTSY— The "*zavolzhskie startsy*" were the "Trans-Volga elders." At a Russian Church Council in 1503 a monk from "across the Volga" attacked the policy of monasteries possessing wealth and land. This monk, Nil Maikov from the Sora hermitage,— known historically as Nil Sorskii (d. 1508)—found support for his position chiefly among the monks from " across the Volga"

["Trans-Volga"]. Since the "*zavolzhskie startsy*" believed that monasteries should not possess wealth or land, they became known as the "non-possessors" ["*nestiazhateli*"]. The chief opponent of the "Trans-Volga elders" was Iosif Sanin, an abbot of a monastery in Volok. Iosif, known historically as St. Joseph of Volokalamsk, believed that the mission of monasticism contained within it a social obligation: monks were to care for the poor, the sick, the downtrodden; they were also required to teach and copy manuscripts. Monasteries had to "possess" money and land to carry out its social mission. Hence the position of Iosif of Volokalamsk became known as the position of the "possessors" ["*stiazhateli*"].

Nil Sorskii and the "*zavolzhskie startsy*" also disagreed with Iosif's position on unrepentent heretics. Iosif believed the Church had the right to call upon the State and, if necessary, use prison and torture on heretics. Nil Sorskii rejected any form of force or violence against heretics. Both Nil Sorskii and Iosif of Volokalamsk were canonized.

ZEMSHCHINA – When Ivan the Terrible created the *oprichnina*, the part of the realm not controlled by the *oprichnina* was known as the *zemshchina*. While the *oprichnina* was the personal government of the Tsar, the *zemshchina* continued to be controlled by the boyars. The *zemshchina* suffered violence at the hands of the *oprichniki*.

ZEMSKII SOBOR – Literally the term means "the landed council" or an assembly at which all the land is represented, or the "national assembly." Some claim the first such assembly was convoked by Ivan the Terrible in 1549-1550, although the topic is controversial.

ZERN' – In Muscovite Russia, where gambling was prohibited, *zern'* was dice used in gambling. A *zernshchik* was a gambler.

ZHALOVANNAIA GRAMOTA – A *zhalovannaia gramota* was a "charter" which could bestow rights, properties, or immunities.

Index